Mathew Scott

Fighting Giants:

A History of Central European Paramilitaries and Their Future in the Era of Hybrid War

Fighting Giants:

A History of Central European Paramilitaries and Their Future in the Era of Hybrid War

Mathew Scott

2022

Carola Hartmann Miles-Verlag Berlin

Bibliografische Information der Deutschen Nationalbibliothek
Die Deutsche Nationalbibliothek verzeichnet diese Publikation in der Deutschen Nationalbibliografie; detaillierte bibliografische Daten sind im Internet über www.dnb.de abrufbar.

© 2022 Carola Hartmann Miles-Verlag, Berlin
www.miles-verlag.jimdo.com
E-Mail: miles-verlag@t-online.de

Herstellung: Books on Demand, Norderstedt

Printed in Germany

ISBN 978-3-96776-034-7

TABLE OF CONTENTS

I.   INTRODUCTION

The post–Cold War order has seen a rise in nationalism and a changing face of military organization in Europe. The phenomenon is manifest since the Crimean invasion of 2014.[1] In the aftermath, a diversity of opinion has proliferated about how Central European governments view paramilitary activity. Each state has a rich nationalist paramilitary tradition dating back 100 years to the interwar period and beyond. The far-right political movement heavily influences each paramilitary case in reaction to socialist or Bolshevik revolutionaries of the period. Therefore, these countries provide a valuable point for comparison in civil-military relations (CMR), hybrid warfare strategies, and how to optimize paramilitary groups for security purposes given political volatility since 2014.

The research indicates Central European states should demarcate paramilitary qualities conducive to state leadership as changes in European defensive arrangements mean they will be more self-regarding and the paramilitaries more essential after American retrenchment. Russia heads into demographic collapse, economic insolvency, and political incoherence making the Kremlin prone to disruption strategies. The two trends reinforce the need for good governance amid Central Europe's changes toward a more militarized society and absolutist military thinking.

The major research questions at hand are, first: How is the far-right movement endangering the state's monopoly on violence and changing the civil-military relationship? Second and more directly, with the likely increase in paramilitarism in the future, how can the German, Polish, and Swedish governments implement effective policy to prevent the growth of malignant, dangerous variants of paramilitarism

---

[1] Steven Lee Myers and Ellen Barry, "Putin Reclaims Crimea for Russia and Bitterly Denounces the West," New York Times, March 18, 2014, sec. World, https://www.nytimes.com/2014/03/19/world/europe/ukraine.html.

while reinforcing potential sources of paramilitary strength leading to an improved security situation to meet contemporary threats?

A. SIGNIFICANCE OF THE RESEARCH QUESTION

Although paramilitaries are not usually a prominent feature in formal security cooperation, they can provide benefits if well managed. For example, Sweden has a civil defense force that integrates large population swaths into contingency security plans. The fact that Sweden benefits from its civil defense force suggests North Atlantic Treaty Organization (NATO) members might also benefit from them. The problems driving a rethinking of European security are a revisionist Russia, an immigration crisis, and a rise in populist right parties in Europe.[2] Germany, Poland, and Sweden are a good lens through which to examine the issues because each has a national populist party providing rhetoric enabling extremist paramilitaries contrary to European integrationist efforts, while simultaneously having embraced successful integrationist projects like the European Union (EU).

The Central European states must mitigate present internal threats. They can help by close examinations of practices and policies constructed for each state's constitutional constraints and security threats. Clearly, some demarcation and decisions must be made by the European states with what to do with the rise of right-wing paramilitarism, as it is highly unlikely paramilitary forces can be eradicated completely. By understanding these three cases alongside the relevant research, prudent policy recommendations for individualized state strategy to the paramilitary question are offered.

---

2 Bojan Bugaric, "Europe's Nationalist Threat," The American Prospect, May 18, 2016, https://prospect.org/api/content/a08f230d-4c80-55cb-954e-7a76315ab26e/.

B. LITERATURE REVIEW

This study engages four broad realms of relevant scholarship on the paramilitary security challenge to and in contemporary Europe: civil-military relations, paramilitarism, historical context, and the role of NATO. Civil-military relations examine a democracy's civilian authority mechanism over a more powerful but subservient military force. This conversation revolves around the elements contributing to civil-military synchronicity, where a lot is written about how civilians can guide state defense structure. Second, are the paramilitary and militia conversations exploring paramilitarism's effect on the state and security. The literature is dense with examples of pro-government paramilitary's impact on helping or hurting dependent on its fundamental makeup: strong versus fragile states, semi-official versus informal organization, and local versus roaming groups. Third is a brief historical overview of Europe from the interwar period to the present but with greater emphasis on the period since 2014. The major events help explain the intangible forces, which influence policy, such as invasion paranoia, political subversion, and nationalism. Fourth is a summary of how the greatest military alliance of all time, NATO, is coping with the developments.

1. Civil-Military Relations Literature

Civil-military relations have been discussed since Clausewitz formulated the trinity of people, the army, and the government with an interaction between each.[3] Some argue that Clausewitz advocates for subjective control of the military by the state government to solve the civil-military problématique where a military's power and efficacy are

---

3 Carl von Clausewitz, On War, trans. Michael Eliot Howard and Peter Paret, Revised ed. Edition (Princeton, N.J: Princeton University Press, 1989).

so great that it can assert direct control over the nation.[4] Some of the classic civil-military theorists, Huntington and Janowitz, offer insights into the civil-military challenge in the three European democracies. Whether to control or minimize the civil-military differences is one way to clarify possible solutions. On the one hand, Huntington's *The Soldier and the State* acknowledges the conservative military versus liberal society trope he suggests a professionalization of the officer corps controls.[5] Since military professionals are experts on the use of violence, civilians should provide objectives the professionals figure out how to achieve with a minimum role for civil authority. Huntington suggests that too much civilian control weakens the military, but too little allows for a coup d'état. The optimal level of control must be negotiated because civilians lack the strategic insights needed to make the most effective use of military force to achieve the grand strategy, which at the time was an error in analysis that became more apparent in the 21st century.

On the other hand, the Janowitzian school has popularity because civilian leaders establish control through the molding of the officer corps into something that reflects society at large.[6] The sociologist properly saw how armies in the 20th century had become major forces in politics, and his theory better interpreted this process than did Huntington. One method for increasing civilian control is choosing military professionals from two camps that emerged from the U.S. armed

---

4 John Binkley, "Clausewitz and Subjective Civilian Control: An Analysis of Clausewitz's Views on the Role of the Military Advisor in the Development of National Policy," Armed Forces & Society 42, no. 2 (April 1, 2016): 251–75, https://doi.org/10.1177/0095327X15594450.

5 Samuel P. Huntington, The Soldier and the State: The Theory and Politics of Civil–Military Relations, Revised edition (Cambridge, Mass: Belknap Press: An Imprint of Harvard University Press, 1981).

6 Morris Janowitz, The Professional Soldier: A Social and Political Portrait, Reissue edition (New York: Free Press, 2017).

forces in WW II: absolutists and pragmatists.[7] The pragmatists fought in the European theatre and learned compromise to keep the battle line intact and fight the limited war with limited support.[8] The absolutists fought a ruthless total war in the Pacific and wanted to end the battles as quickly as possible by any means necessary.[9] Janowitz favored the American Cold War pragmatists, but each war's unique nature results in different mentalities rising to the top via civilian selection.[10] Another helpful concept Janowitz constructed was the republic progressing down one of two paths, the militarization of society or a civilianization of the military. Janowitz suggests that the latter is optimal, for which professional soldiers abhorred him. The method for the civilization of the military is through broad, far-reaching conscription with an all-inclusive officer ascension program drawn from the system of U.S. colleges as well as from the enlisted ranks without undue regard for social privilege. The militarization-civilianization axis, combined with the absolutist-pragmatist axis, is a helpful way to explore civil-military relations for these states.

There are more too civil-military relations as different thinkers add nuances to the discussion. Max Weber writes that "a state is a human community that (successfully) claims the monopoly of the legitimate use of force within a given territory."[11] Weber's conception of state-dominated violence reaches a zenith during Cold War fears of a nuclear exchange and then fades as Cold War peace yields to the current multipolar world of self-help. Russia's recent employment of hybrid warfare as a form of total war is challenging liberal democracies

---

7 Andrew Hacker, "The Professional Soldier, by Morris Janowitz," Commentary Magazine, September 1, 1960, https://www.commentary.org/articles/andrew-hacker/the-professional-soldier-by-morris-janowitz/.
8 Hacker.
9 Hacker.
10 Hacker.
11 Max Weber, Hans Heinrich Gerth, and C. Wright Mills, From Max Weber: Essays in Sociology (Ulan Press, 2012).

with separatist and extremist elements latent in the population. There-fore, Strachan and Ruth reflect that societal resilience in security and defense must be a goal for established democratic states and public en-gagement with the military structure was a way to accomplish the goal.[12] Matei and Halladay show that democratic governments expect an ef-fective military to counter threats in a more multipolar world.[13] They link a positive democratic civil-military relationship with good inter-military-civilian relations, which mutual knowledge, institutions with effective processes, and a dedication to democratic norms in the mili-tary community to make this happen. Furthermore, Matei and Halladay recommend transparency, accountability, and dialogue as essential in an iterative process between the two, which strives for a workable bal-ance.

In Germany, CMR are stable, but the Alternative for Germany (Alternative für Deutschland or AfD), a far-right populist party, seeks to peel the *Bundeswehr* (Germany's army) away from the German Basic Law to re-establish aspects of the old militarism, as Abenheim's re-search indicates.[14] Moldovan found Polish CMR fixates on Russia since the invasion of Crimea, so Poland is building regional military capacity

---

12 Hew Strachan and Ruth Harris, "The Utility of Military Force and Public Under-standing in Today's Britain" (Rand Corporation, April 16, 2020), https://www.rand.org/pubs/research_reports/RRA213-1.html.
13 Florina Cristiana Matei and Carolyn Halladay, "The Control-Effectiveness Frame-work of Civil–Military Relations," Oxford Research Encyclopedia of Politics, Febru-ary 23, 2021, https://doi.org/10.1093/acrefore/9780190228637.013.1874.
14 Donald Abenheim, "Bundeswehr and Alternative Für Deutschland (AfD): 'Die Soldatenpartei'? [Bundeswehr and Alternative For Germany (AfD): 'The Soldiers Party'?]," in Jahrbuch Innere Führung 2019, ed. Uwe Hartmann and Claus von Rosen, vol. 2019, 2 vols., 2019, 392, https://www.bod.de/buchshop/jahrbuch-innere-fueh-rung-2019-9783945861981.

in addition, advocating its needs to NATO.[15] Holmberg explores Swedish politics and society in rethinking its demilitarization after the Soviet collapse, and a trend towards remilitarization is developing.[16] Another common theme is that paramilitaries are a challenge to the state, and open dialogue between military commanders and civilians is essential.

2.   Paramilitary and Militia Literature

According to scholars, paramilitaries, militias, state defense forces, and other irregular units are an important consideration in the cost-benefit analysis for the post-2014 state of total-war thinking. This thesis defines paramilitaries and militias, civil defense forces, and their analogs as ideologically driven, politically active groups, organized by hierarchy, drilling in military tactics but are not necessarily armed with firearms, sometimes using informal insignia or uniforms. Therefore, paramilitary groups may exist on a spectrum from civilian to military. But some distinctions must be made to characterize each group better. Carey and Mitchell place these organizations into two groups, semi-official versus informal.[17] The two bins have implications for societies where these irregular forces exist.[18] Ahram views paramilitaries as proxy forces the state tolerates for lack of better options or due to their low

15 Anton-Gabriel Moldovan, "Poland's National Security Policy in a New Regional Security Environment. Case Study: National Security Strategy of Poland (2014)," Toruńskie Studia Międzynarodowe 1, no. 11 (2018): 89–102.

16 Arita Holmberg, "A Demilitarization Process under Challenge? The Example of Sweden," Defense Studies 15, no. 3 (July 3, 2015): 235–53, https://doi.org/10.1080/14702436.2015.1084174.

17 Sabine C. Carey and Neil J. Mitchell, "Progovernment Militias," Annual Review of Political Science Vol. 20 (May 2017): 127–47.

18 Sabine C. Carey and Neil J. Mitchell, "Progovernment Militias," Annual Review of Political Science 20, no. 1 (2017): 127–47, https://doi.org/10.1146/annurev-polisci-051915-045433.

overall cost for security.[19] Bapat suggests border security is augmented with paramilitary forces of the semi-official and informal variety.[20]

There is a proclivity for security-focused paramilitary groups that have little oversight but with access to weapons to "turn bad" if not under supervision, according to Schuberth.[21] Therefore, Staniland holds that a better understanding of the paramilitary-state relationship must consider the role of ideology in any discussion pertaining to politics and potential political violence.[22] The paramilitary literature provides valid suggestions for policymakers in the three states.

The state can become aware of traits that demonstrate a paramilitary's inclinations. Campbell and Brenner show that the political-paramilitary connection leading to death squads is sometimes facilitated by the government when incentives are aligned, even in the developed world. If paramilitary groups are populated with veterans or off-duty military, then they tend to be more brutal, secretive, selective, and have a greater capacity for violence.[23] A challenge for democratizing states and those with strong historical ties to paramilitarism means the paramilitary units harm rather than help states who have a tenuous grasp

19 Ariel Ahram, Proxy Warriors: The Rise and Fall of State-Sponsored Militias, 1st edition (Stanford, Calif: Stanford Security Studies, 2011).
20 Navin A. Bapat, "Understanding State Sponsorship of Militant Groups," British Journal of Political Science 42, no. 1 (2012): 1–29.
21 Moritz Schuberth, "The Challenge of Community-Based Armed Groups: Towards a Conceptualization of Militias, Gangs, and Vigilantes," Contemporary Security Policy 36, no. 2 (May 4, 2015): 296–320, https://doi.org/10.1080/13523260.2015.1061756.
22 Paul Staniland, "Militias, Ideology, and the State," Journal of Conflict Resolution 59, no. 5 (August 1, 2015): 770–93, https://doi.org/10.1177/0022002715576749.
23 Bruce Campbell and Arthur Brenner, eds., Death Squads in Global Perspective: Murder with Deniability (Palgrave Macmillan US, 2000), https://doi.org/10.1057/9780230108141.

on the monopoly of violence within their borders as inexpensive weapons proliferate, according to Pereira.[24] Bates says paramilitary action may anticipate state failure, yet in some instances, paramilitaries add stability to state security.[25] Finally, Miller finds that a semi-official variant offers advantages to the state as an increase in linkage and security goals allow for more accountability and mitigate extremism in the paramilitary ranks.[26] Ultimately, an overall theme is that security is the state's responsibility, and its military force must reconcile with overarching security structures to achieve democratic ends.

3. European Politics Literature

The Russian invasion of Crimea, along with mass migration and the rise of right-wing parties, tests the European commitment to an ever-greater union. Polling shows that the migrant crisis concerns Europeans with lawlessness and is a source of Islamic terrorism after the 2015 attacks.[27] Following the migrant crisis and terror attacks, right-wing extreme nationalist parties are increasing their government representation from 2015 onward, for example, Germany's AfD, Poland's Law and Peace (PiS), and the Sweden Democrats (SD).[28] The populists

24 Anthony Pereira, "Armed Forces, Coercive Monopolies, and Changing Patterns of State Formation and Violence," January 1, 2003, 387–408, https://doi.org/10.1017/CBO9780511510038.016.

25 Robert H. Bates, When Things Fell Apart: State Failure in Late-Century Africa, Illustrated edition (New York: Cambridge University Press, 2008).

26 Gary J. Miller, "The Political Evolution of Principal-Agent Models," Annual Review of Political Science 8, no. 1 (June 15, 2005): 203–25, https://doi.org/10.1146/annurev.polisci.8.082103.104840.

27 Rukmini Callimachi, "ISIS Claims Responsibility, Calling Paris Attacks 'First of the Storm,'" The New York Times, November 14, 2015, sec. World, https://www.nytimes.com/2015/11/15/world/europe/isis-claims-responsibility-for-paris-attacks-calling-them-miracles.html.

28 Charles Lees, "The 'Alternative for Germany': The Rise of Right-Wing Populism at the Heart of Europe," Politics, June 4, 2018, https://doi.org/10.1177/0263395718777718.

question the presumptions of the European Union's values: cosmopolitanism, liberalism, and European integration.[29] The populists also tend to support each other, despite their typically nationalist focus, as they have common interests.[30]

These parties have recharged nationalist rhetoric of blood and soil, which, in turn, encourages more extreme elements in society as they find their way into extremist paramilitary forces.[31] Each instance of paramilitarism correlates with different circumstances, but the political landscape of late is mainly enabling. The 21st-century phenomenon of so-called "hybrid warfare" in Ukraine or Syria allows paramilitaries to act in an actual conflict, reinforcing the paramilitaries' resolve and capability.[32] A phenomenon emerges where paramilitary recruitment and extremism grows in otherwise peaceful, prosperous European countries that are ever more beset by conflict. Of concern are the implications paramilitary opportunities have for regular European civil-military defense structures, which must grapple with citizens in their dozens who have joined the ranks of extremist groups and see militia and irregular soldiering as a panacea in crisis.

4. NATO Response to Paramilitaries

NATO is perhaps even less suited to combat far-right extremist activity when framed as domestic terrorists who do not exceed interstate intervention efforts. In 2014, NATO addressed paramilitary

29 "The Right-Wing Nationalists Shaking Up Europe," BBC News, November 13, 2019, https://www.bbc.com/news/world-europe-36130006.
30 Tamás Boros et al., "The State of Populism in Europe" (Foundation for European Progressive Studies, 2016).
31 Florian Bieber, "How Europe's Nationalists Became Internationalists," Foreign Policy, November 30, 2019, https://foreignpolicy.com/2019/11/30/how-europes-nationalists-became-internationalists/.
32 Jeffery Herbst, "War and the State in Africa," International Security 14, no. 4 (1990): 117–39.

threats vis-a-vis Russia and Ukraine but, it has failed to dedicate sufficient thought and resources to the domestic, right-wing extremist variety. The 2014 Wales North Atlantic Council summit suggests standing
up the Very High Readiness Joint Task Force of 5,000 soldiers with an
augmentation of up to 30,000 airmen, sailors, and special forces available with its Readiness Action Plan.[33] The NATO website recommends
that the targeted state has primary responsibility for response with
NATO prepared to assist.[34] With the threat of subversion and subterfuge so prominent after the Crimean Anschluss, NATO's Joint Intelligence and Security Division (JISD) started in 2016 to support the
North Atlantic Council and Military Committee in decision making.[35]
In 2017, the Helsinki-based European Center of Excellence for Countering Hybrid Threats began as a think tank to support NATO and EU
efforts.[36]

The U.S.-based RAND Corporation is another think tank publishing on NATO and hybrid war. One report concerning Russia as a
threat mentions Russia targeting European elections to influence them
to the Kremlin's benefit.[37] In one instance, Russia might have tried to
oust Angela Merkel during reelection in 2017, so the contingent of pro-
Moscow in the center-left Social Democratic Party candidate would
win. RAND scholars suggest four strategies to counter Russia. First,

33 NATO, "Readiness Action Plan," NATO, accessed May 27, 2021,
http://www.nato.int/cps/en/natohq/topics_119353.htm.
34 NATO, "NATO's Response to Hybrid Threats," NATO, accessed May 27, 2021,
http://www.nato.int/cps/en/natohq/topics_156338.htm.
35 NATO, "Joint Intelligence and Security (JIS) Division," NATO, accessed May 27,
2021, http://www.nato.int/cps/en/natolive/107942.htm.
36 European Centre of Excellence for Countering Hybrid Threats, "What Is Hybrid
CoE," Hybrid CoE - The European Centre of Excellence for Countering Hybrid
Threats, accessed May 27, 2021, https://www.hybridcoe.fi/who-what-and-how/.
37 Christopher Chivvis, Understanding Russian "Hybrid Warfare": And What Can
Be Done About It (Rand Corporation, 2017), https://doi.org/10.7249/CT468.

efficient U.S. interagency unity in action is necessary between Intelligence communities, and State, Defense, Treasury departments. Second, maintaining optimal funding for intelligence collection and analysis in European security policy. Third, the U.S. can do much to support Europe in its fight against hybrid warfare, so it should do so. Fourth, Europe must find ways to fight the propaganda outlet, Russia Today, and other disinformation media once more so prominent in Russian statecraft as in former times. These are useful support mechanisms, but NATO, as with its focus on the strategic level of security, defense, and military affairs, is less suited for the below-the-threshold-of-war strategy of hybrid warfare.

C.   POTENTIAL EXPLANATIONS AND HYPOTHESES

Paramilitaries can be a vector to spread extremist thinking where guerilla training in Russia or immigrant hunting is an outcome. A hypothesis is that including would-be white patriots into a state-operated paramilitary might be a decisive factor in reducing their size, influence, and radicalism. The states that create semi-official paramilitary will have fewer symptoms of military extremism than that of other states prosecuting paramilitary organizations into an underground. The semi-official model would prevent paramilitary members from fighting in conflicts abroad by instituting membership requirements that preclude such activity. Eradication and authoritarian control alone are unlikely to yield satisfactory results.

State policies are a promising area of research for coopting the aspiring militarist in society and putting these aspirants on a path, which benefits state security. The German, Polish, and Swedish cases were chosen to illustrate two models: states that incorporate paramilitaries into defense (semiofficial) and states with unofficial paramilitaries (informal). The Polish model incorporates paramilitaries into the defense structure while Sweden's Home Guard is a multirole reserve force under the defense ministry, so these represent the semiofficial version. Germany does not have a paramilitary branch of its defense forces, so its paramilitary remains an anti-state, far-right club.

The key assumptions embedded in the case comparisons are tied to EU and NATO participation requirements, which all three countries share except Sweden not being a NATO member. But the EU conditions for membership, otherwise known as the Copenhagen criteria, are relevant here; countries are expected to be a stable democracy, have human rights with respect for and protection of minority rights, and an obligation/capacity to institute political, economic, and monetary requirements.[38] The shared expectations allow some comparison within a democratic framework. The democratic governments in these countries form an essential facet for commonality, as each should be following the same norms and practices by treaty at some basic level.

D.   RESEARCH DESIGN

The research explores case studies relevant to instances where government policy improves overall security by minimizing extremist right-wing paramilitaries in addition to supplementing the conventional military structure with self-defense forces or home guards. The case study looks at top-down state influence on paramilitarism activity versus bottom-up ideological challenges from the far-right movement. Janowitz provides the construct for examining civil-military relations. Pro-government militia literature offers best practices where discrepancies exist in individual cases. This research uses qualitative case studies of history, military policy, and defense analysis to illustrate how

---

38 "EU Conditions for Membership," Text, European Neighbourhood Policy And Enlargement Negotiations - European Commission, December 6, 2016, https://ec.europa.eu/neighbourhood-enlargement/policy/conditions-membership_en.

democratic civil-military relations today can influence and improve states' relationship to paramilitarism among their population. Qualitative case studies offer the best approach to exploring the naturally occurring phenomenon through several data sources. The materials used for this research will draw from scholarly journals, books, government documents, white papers, official websites, online newspaper articles, and social media postings. Official websites and social media are relevant because it gives paramilitary organizations a voice in their own words, which may be helpful in recruitment and counter strategy.

1.   THESIS OVERVIEW AND DRAFT CHAPTER OUTLINE

The thesis organization follows a standard format. Chapter I is the introduction chapter with the major research question presented and its importance, problems, hypothesis, methods, and an overview. Chapter II examines German paramilitary history to the present with a concentration on the 2014 episode onwards and then official response policies. Chapter III is an examination of Polish paramilitary history. Chapter IV is an examination of Swedish paramilitary history. Chapter V is a qualitative case study of the three countries as they bare on the results of the variables considered with comparisons made between outcomes and an overall conclusion. This organization lays out the facts in each state for comparison and determination of prudent measures.

II.   GERMANY

Germany signifies the country in Europe where, in the past, the role of the paramilitary in politics culminated in the greatest political mass murder of the continent since the Thirty Years War. For decades, the nation has also embodied reasonably sound democratic civil-military relations in which the former ills of paramilitary formations in domestic politics have played no role. Today, however, the German paramilitary case shows two alarming trends without much assurance that things will improve in the near future: Russian revision of the Central European order and European federal disintegration. Nazi paramilitary violence is imitated well into the 21st century by Europe's right-wing against real or perceived threats. Germany's counterrevolutionary, nationalistic paramilitary is synonymous with the patriotic struggle against supranational integrationist forces and their cosmopolitan values in the EU and NATO. After the 2014 Crimean invasion by "little green men," i.e., Russian special forces and shock troops, a drawn-out low-intensity war has plagued the Donbas region of East Ukraine. In 2015, the European migration crisis burst upon an EU that had neglected mass movements of people as a security issue. This combination of pressure and problems allowed the neo-Nazi and extreme nationalist parties to make new electoral gains in Germany's upturned political scene.

The Crimean invasion and the migration crisis also led to a shocking revival of paramilitary activity in Germany, one embedded into the German security sector itself and one where German civilian paramilitary freebooters are active in the Ukrainian and Syrian conflict zones. These paramilitarists return home radicalized and stoke nationalism in the military, government institutions, and society. More is at plan than simple nationalistic fervor within the voting box. The rise of the paramilitarists and their supporting political movement have consequences for Germany's strategic interests in European federalism and

Russian resurgence.[39] Both are symptoms of returned integral nationalism, that is, violent blood and soil nationalism, which the populist-right, paramilitarists, and far-right military members are promoting to undermine Germany's constitutional order and its formerly secure place in a peaceful Europe. This upheaval at home and abroad is providing in 2021 an opportunity for Russia to undermine the German strength in constitutions and statecraft.

A.   PARAMILITARY HISTORY

In 1918, defeat in war gave rise to a civil-military cosmos in central Europe in which paramilitary entities took hold quickly with eventual catastrophic results. The post-WW I *Freikorps* (irregular military echelons recruited from soldiers who did not demobilize) best illustrated German paramilitary duality. The Freikorps was composed of returning WW I veterans and were used by the new Socialist-led government in an emergency capacity despite their anti-liberal, militaristic tendencies in the newly founded democracy. According to Robert Waite, Germany's relevant paramilitary events began after WW I and the power vacuum that ensued, which fostered a powerful Freikorps paramilitary.[40] The war's termination left Germany in a precarious position in several ways. The German General Staff assessed that the army tenuously held the Western Front, so they began the armistice process.[41] The German political apparatus and the General Staff realized a more representative government should be installed according to the

39 France-Presse Agence, "AFD Party Votes to Campaign for German Exit from EU," Guardian, January 13, 2019, https://www.theguardian.com/world/2019/jan/13/afd-party-to-campaign-for-german-exit-from-european-union.
40 Robert G. L. Waite, Vanguard of Nazism: The Free Corps Movement in Postwar Germany, 1918-1923 (Harvard University Press, 1952), https://www.hup.harvard.edu/catalog.php?isbn=9780674931428.
41 Randal Gray and Christopher Argyle, Chronicle of the First World War: Volume II - 1917-1921 (New York: Facts on File Inc., New York, 1991).

allies' Fourteen point plan to expedite the war's end.[42] Notably, the Fourteen point plan contained clauses for a greatly reduced German military, a reversal of Franco-Prussian War gains, and Polish autonomy of formerly German lands. Kaiser Wilhelm II abdicated under those terms creating the Weimar Republic.[43] These events allowed the Freikorps to rise and react to the unfolding chaos.

The Weimar Republic had a difficult transition to democracy, which the Freikorps was expedient in putting down the Soviet-style threat to the new state. Mutiny started in the German navy and spread into the large cities as the General Staff attempted to end the war.[44] The 1918 Russian Revolution also began to inspire German socialists to agitate for further social and political change. The new Weimar government struggled to quell the Berlin paramilitary revolutionaries during the Spartacist Uprising of 6 January.[45] At the same time, homecoming veterans contributed to the instability. The Treaty of Versailles forced the new army into a five-fold reduction in manpower after the war. Massive unemployment among veterans meant that they found work in the Freikorps.[46] Another issue that drove instability was the stab-in-the-back myth being cultivated in the unseated officer caste and paramilitary cadre. The stab-in-the-back myth was an anti-Semitic conspiracy theory that suggested Germany was not defeated on the battlefields but rather through social and political subversion perpetrated by Jews, socialists, and republicans, causing civil collapse.[47] The new democratic government was *bête noire* for right-wing extremists who blamed it for

---

42 Gray and Argyle.
43 Gray and Argyle.
44 Travis, Paramilitary Organizations in Germany from 1871-1945.
45 Mark Jones, Founding Weimar: Violence and the German Revolution of 1918–1919 (Cambridge, United Kingdom: Cambridge University Press, 2016).
46 Travis, Paramilitary Organizations in Germany from 1871-1945.
47 Ian Kershaw, To Hell and Back: Europe 1914-1949 (The Penguin History of Europe) (Penguin Books, 2016), https://www.amazon.com/Hell-Back-1914-1949-Penguin-History/dp/0143109928.

Germany's surrender and failure to handle a range of social and political problems.[48] The Freikorps quelled the Spartacist Uprising under government direction in 1919, which increased the Freikorps' recruitment.

Expanding Freikorps activity and politicization became a source for later anti-democratic symptoms in the republic. One such symptom left the republic vulnerable to right-wing nationalist putsch. Paramilitary putsches happened with regularity and included the 1920 four-day successful Kapp Putsch in Berlin; a 1920 failed socialist Ruhr Uprising, then an unsuccessful 1923 Beer Hall Putsch organized by Adolf Hitler and WW I commander Erich Ludendorff.[49] The period of brutalized politics in the postwar years meant a continued cycle of conflict, revolt, and counter-revolt where WW I ended, and battle-hardened soldiers became political in the atmosphere of defeat.[50] In fact, up to 400,000 men joined a paramilitary group by 1921.[51] Many members of the Freikorps found common ground with the National Socialist Workers (NSDAP or Nazi) Party under Adolf Hitler.

The Freikorps case showed three trends up to the mid-1920s. First, weakly consolidated democratic institutions failed to stop cycles of radical uprisings and armed paramilitary response to those uprisings, which further eroded democratic strength. Second, the paramilitary took root in society as a semi-legitimate organization for patriotic veterans to secure political outcomes around a nationalist ideology amid a socialist threat. Third, paramilitary activity became a destructive force

---

48 Travis, Paramilitary Organizations in Germany from 1871-1945.

49 Harold J. Gordon, Hitler and the Beer Hall Putsch, 1st edition (Princeton, N.J: Princeton University Press, 1972).

50 Gerwarth, Robert., and John Horne. War in Peace: Paramilitary Violence in Europe after the Great War. 1st ed. Oxford: Oxford University Press, 2012.

51 United States Holocaust Memorial Museum, "The SA," Holocaust Encyclopedia The SA, September 17, 2017, https://encyclopedia.ushmm.org/content/en/article/the-sa.

for a civil society where opposition was met with violence rather than civil discourse.

The period before WW II could be considered the golden age of German paramilitarism due to the high levels of participation, prominence in the chaotic pre-Nazi state, and historical cachet, which many paramilitaries and people on the far-right have since come to imitate across Europe and North America. The most important thread of paramilitary history began with Hitler's release from prison after the failed Beerhall Putsch. Hitler's reintegration into paramilitary politics coincided with a consolidation of paramilitary forces under Nazi party control throughout the 1920s and early 1930s. Freikorps members in Bavaria joined the deceptively named Gymnastic and Sports Division of the Nazi party, which in its turn became the *Sturmabteilung* (Storm Detachment, SA). The SA was the closest to the ideal form of paramilitary structure as, under the guidance of Ernst Roehm, by 1933, it had almost become a duplicate German army without democratic-civilian control except for the Nazi elite, who operated it as a private army.[52] In 1933, newly elected Nazis pursued a path toward legitimacy with a reduced role for the SA, whose growing power might threaten Nazi's control. In particular, former Freikorps-turned-SA Commander Ernst Röhm needed to be eliminated along with the SA's thuggish, brawling reputation.[53] In 1934, the state-controlled *Schutzstaffel* (Protection Squadron, SS), *Sicherheitsdienst* (Security Service, SD), and *Geheimstaats Polizei* (Secret States Police, Gestapo) murdered SA leadership on the Night of the Long Knives.[54] The move greatly reduced the SA as a viable threat and consolidated all right-wing paramilitary forces under state control of the Nazi regime from 1933 until the conclusion of WW II.

---

52 United States Holocaust Memorial Museum.
53 Gordon Craig, The Politics of the Prussian Army, 1640-1945, 1st edition (Oxford University Press, 1956).
54 United States Holocaust Memorial Museum, "The SA."

25

The SA's politicized paramilitary successor, the SS, expanded and refined the SA's illicit duties on a wider, more efficient scale of operations when it oversaw the Holocaust with its *Einsatzgruppen* (specialized terror and killing squads).[55] The Einsatzgruppen would carry out the Holocaust, first with roving rifle gangs and then through the mechanized murder of the death camps. As opposed to the SA, the SS was a highly selective paramilitary that attracted the German social elites to the SS officer cadre, similar to Prussia's mandate for martial service.[56] German paramilitarism prior to and during WW II was varied in tasking and professionalism depending on the organization. For example, in 1938, paramilitaries were front and center for *Kristallnacht's* (Night of Broken Glass) persecution of German Jews.[57] On the other extreme, some 1ˢᵗ tier *Waffen-SS* (Armed SS) units like SS-Panzer-Division "Das Reich" earned 55 percent of the Knights' Crosses awarded to Waffen SS units indicating a high martial proficiency.[58] Unlike the wartime SS, the NSDAP and the disgraced SA created a last-ditch echelon in the *Volkssturm* (People's Storm) paramilitary. The late war German homeland defense fell to elements of the *Volkssturm*, which had very mixed professional expertise and discipline due to the recruitment of men, women, and children otherwise not suited for combat.[59] With much of the Waffen SS having been destroyed amid the withdrawal

---

55 Hugh Trevor-Roper, The Good Old Days: The Holocaust as Seen by Its Perpetrators and Bystanders, ed. Ernst Klee, Willi Dressen, and Volker Riess (William S. Konecky Associates, 1996).
56 Herbert F. Ziegler, Nazi Germany's New Aristocracy: The SS Leadership,1925-1939 (Princeton University Press, 2014).
57 United States Holocaust Memorial Museum, "Kristallnacht," Holocaust Encyclopedia Kristallnacht, October 18, 2019, https://encyclopedia.ushmm.org/content/en/article/kristallnacht.
58 Bernd Wegner, Hitlers Politische Soldaten: Die Waffen-SS 1933 - 1945: Leitbild, Struktur und Funktion einer nationalsozialistischen Elite [Hitler's Political Soldiers: The Waffen-SS 1933-1945: Mission, Structure and Function of a National Socialist Elite], 8th ed. edition (Schoeningh Ferdinand GmbH, 2010).
59 United States Holocaust Memorial Museum, "The SA."

from Eastern Europe, the Volkssturm and the Hitler Youth fought in the doomed effort to defend Berlin against the final Soviet Army envelopment.[60] The paramilitaries of the wartime Third Reich covered a wide range of professionalism and ideological commitment, but the far-right simplified the historical record to suit their aims.

The fanaticism of the Third Reich's total war concept late in the conflict was typified by the Battle of Berlin in the spring of 1945. A combination of armed and unarmed citizens fought alongside children into the final hours.[61] A diminished Waffen-SS was organized beside the Volkssturm until the end of hostilities on 2 May 1945.[62] Another paramilitary tactic of the late Third Reich was Operation *Werwolf*, conceived after D-Day by Josef Goebbels and Martin Bormann, where resistance against the allies would continue after the final surrender.[63] However, German commanders refused to supply weapons needed to support the operation during their retreats, so no significant Nazi insurgency materialized despite Nazi dreams and Allied fears.[64] The Nazi paramilitaries perverted such old Prussian virtues as service, hard work, thrift, and morality. The Freikorps-to-SS transition turned those virtues into a culture of hyper militarism, brutality, and ideological extremism against those blamed for the defeat of Germany after a hard-fought war. Their progressively counterrevolutionary character is evident in their elimination of political challenges to include the Nazis' early paramilitary, the SA, and an attempt by Himmler after 20 July 1944 to

60 David K. Yelton, Hitler's Volkssturm: The Nazi Militia and the Fall of Germany, '44–'45 (Lawrence, KS: Kansas University Press, 2002), 155.
61 Antony Beevor, Berlin: The Downfall, 1945 (New Haven, CN: Penguin Books, Limited, 2010).
62 Beevor.
63 Perry Biddiscombe, The Last Nazis: SS Werewolf Guerrilla Resistance in Europe 1944-1947, 1st Edition (Stroud: Tempus Pub Ltd, 2000).
64 Beevor, Berlin.

supplant the armed forces altogether. Therefore, the SS notion of German paramilitary discredits a tradition dating back to Fredrick the Great by an association with warped, predatory banditry.

Far-right parties morphed alongside extremist criminal activity despite efforts by the postwar democratic establishment to offer a better way forward. German defeat coupled with a postwar denazification stood down the existing paramilitary units and outlawed them in the western Federal Republic of Germany. The promulgation of the Basic Law, as West Germany's constitution was called, in 1949 affirmed democratic governance, the rule of law, and a prohibition of anti-democratic practices and parties.[65] The Basic Laws' article 86a outlawed the "use of symbols of unconstitutional organizations."[66] German extremism expert Gerard Braunthal states that several Nazi-successor parties were banned from 1950 onward under the Federal Republic of Germany's Basic Law, including the Socialist Reich Party (SRP) and the German Reich Party.[67] But, the far-right parties continued their extremist criminal activity in an initially stronger and then in a more restrained posture.

The banishment of German far-right, anti-constitutional parties in the 1950s tested democratic consolidation as many former Nazis attempted to restyle the ideology in the Bonn Republic. Those excluded parties had troublesome connections with former Wehrmacht officer

---

65 Federal Republic of Germany, "Basic Law," accessed May 12, 2021, https://www.bundesregierung.de/breg-en/chancellor/basic-law-470510.
66 Andreas Stegbauer, "The Ban of Right-Wing Extremist Symbols According to Section 86a of the German Criminal Code," German Law Journal 8, no. 2 (February 1, 2007): 173–84, https://doi.org/10.1017/S2071832200005496.
67 Gerard Braunthal, Right-Wing Extremism in Contemporary Germany, 2009th edition (Basingstoke, UK ; New York: Palgrave Macmillan, 2009),https://www.amazon.com/Right-Wing-Extremism-Contemporary-Perspectives-Political/dp/0230236391/ref=sr_1_2?dchild=1&keywords=extremism+in+contemporary+germany&qid=1617994132&sr=8-2.

Hans-Ulrich Rudel and SS officer, Leo von Jena, as their motive figures.[68] Both men had pre-war paramilitary membership. These far-right parties recreated a bad imitation of the Hitler Youth in the SRP's Reich Youth and Viking Youth. Youth branches were networking forums for right-wing extremism among those involved. Some reckoning came when the center-right Christian Democratic Union (CDU)/Christian Social Union (CSU) made overtures to the former Nazis to build faith in democratic practice following the SRP's ban.[69] Far-right parties continued to develop throughout the Cold War period, such as the National Democratic Party of Germany, Free Workers Party, and later the Republicans, with various connections to former Nazis.

The post-war far-right party's reanimation had continuity with the pre-war German counterrevolutionary sentiment. The Holocaust and Hitler's destruction orders did not form an insurmountable barrier for those who would channel those politics for action in the Federal Republic well past the Third Reich's collapse. Center-right parties attempted to offer them small-scale compromises but were rejected in favor of more radical, anti-democratic parties. There may be a cyclical relationship between paramilitary and politics where parties grow the rank-and-file paramilitary membership through rhetoric, and paramilitary members support the parties at the ballot box. The civil challenge of far-right parties is not easily solved because the far-right's violent blood and soil dogma cannot be ameliorated with good economic or defense policy.

The Cold War tension maintained aspects of total war by militarizing large subsets of the population against the old communist and Soviet foes. Allied planning for irregular warfare in the face of a Soviet

---

68 Daniel Siemens, Stormtroopers: A New History of Hitler's Brownshirts (Yale University Press, 2017).
69 Braunthal, Right-Wing Extremism in Contemporary Germany.

assault meant that the formal defense apparatus of the Cold War restarted elements of clandestine German paramilitary in partnership with NATO's Office of Security, the CIA, and British MI6 known as Operation *Gladio* (Sword).[70] Gladio began around 1948 when anti-communists, many of whom were former SS, were trained in guerilla tactics/hybrid war tasked with hunting communists in the Reich and filled the ranks for the same purpose.[71] The International Military Tribunal spared such useful former Nazis as Klaus Barbie to facilitate Operation Gladio's recruitment of other Nazis.[72] The employment of certain and select high-profile Nazis in the security system was known by President Harry Truman and West German Chancellor Konrad Adenauer alike, and they agreed to hold off persecutions of certain right-wing extremists when Germany joined NATO in 1955.[73] Operation Gladio represented an attempt at paramilitary networks across Europe that was, in fact, part of the western defense pact and its hybrid war operations of the late 1940s into the 1960s—a fact that is often lost in many accounts of said conflict.

Right-wing paramilitary activity found further sponsorship in the CIA as a bulwark against communism. By 1959, Operation Gladio's small, secret paramilitary resistance force expanded across Europe, including the neutral countries, i.e., Austria, to conduct surveillance and sabotage in case of Soviet invasion of western Europe.[74] However, the stay-behind networks proliferated beyond German knowledge with the CIA's encouragement of Bund Deutscher Jugend's Technisher Dienst

---

70 Clare Pedrick, "CIA Organized Secret Army In Western Europe," Washington Post, November 14, 1990, https://www.washingtonpost.com/archive/politics/1990/11/14/cia-organized-secret-army-in-western-europe/e0305101-97b9-4494-bc18-d89f42497d85/.
71 NATO's Secret Armies: Operation Gladio and Terrorism in Western Europe (Routledge, 2005), https://doi.org/10.4324/9780203017777.
72 NATO's Secret Armies.
73 NATO's Secret Armies.
74 NATO's Secret Armies.

(Association of German Youth's Technical Service), also known as LCPROWL.[75] The service consisted of anti-communist paramilitary resistance training. These networks showed how the clandestine services were willing to accommodate the far-right to achieve an operational goal beyond the frame of the democratic clauses of the Basic Law.

Another feature of the West German landscape was the military sports groups operating as paramilitary gangs. For example, by 1978, the Rohwer group attacked a Dutch contingent of NATO at a military training facility in Bergenfahne, Germany.[76] The former East German Karl-Heinz Hoffman led another group in the 1970s known as *Wehrsportgruppe Hoffmann*.[77] The Hoffman group conducted paramilitary training for hundreds of people using neo-Nazi principles for coup d'état preparation in Europe. As the turmoil in the Middle East joined with subterfuge in Central Europe, the Hoffman group moved to Lebanon to work alongside the Palestine Liberation Organization to conduct terrorism against the state of Israel.[78] These actions made the Hoffman group highly regarded in right-wing extremist circles, and it was a template others followed, such as the Military Sports Group *Werwolf*.[79] By the 1970s and 1980s, West Germany witnessed increased skinhead culture, with neo-Nazi gangs harassing southern European guest

---

75 "Project: LCPROWL," Nazi War Crimes Disclosure Act (Washington, DC: Central Intelligence Agency, 2007), https://www.cia.gov/readingroom/docs/LCPROWL%20%20%20%20VOL.%201_0036.pdf.

76 "Panzer Von Links [Tanks From The Left]," Der Spiegel, May 14, 1978, https://www.spiegel.de/politik/panzer-von-links-a-98db3653-0002-0001-0000-000040615444.

77 Daniel Koehler, Right-Wing Terrorism in the 21st Century: The 'National Socialist Underground' and the History of Terror from the Far-Right in Germany, 1st edition (London New York: Routledge, 2018).

78 Andrea Röpke and Andreas Speit, Blut und Ehre: Geschichte und Gegenwart Rechter Gewalt in Deutschland [Blood and Honor : Past and Present of Right-Wing Violence in Germany] (Ch. Links Verlag, 2013).

79 Olaf Sundermeyer, Right-Wing Terror in Germany: A History of Violence (München: Beck CH, 2012).

workers who competed with Germany's urban working class for jobs.[80] The military sports groups represented a serious threat to German authorities, while the skinheads were typically disorganized hooligans.

As Germany transitioned to the post–Cold War 1990s, the now unnecessary anti-Soviet networks resurfaced. Initially, the stay-behind networks were built when West Germany had no army, so the networks were thought to have been previously dismantled by the German Federal Intelligence Service. However, in 1995, a neo-Nazi named Peter Nauman led police and media cameras to 13 separate arms caches with hundreds of kilograms of ammunition and explosives.[81] The Cold War grey zone security forces signify continued usage of its right-wing paramilitarism to defend against revolutionary expansion and a widening gap between paramilitary and civilian structure in the CIA's sponsorship of undemocratically supervised armed right-wing.

Setting Operation Gladio and its anti-Soviet networks aside, the Cold War paramilitarists offered a clue to their motivation where right-wing extremists' initiative is fighting the left without civilian oversight. The paramilitarists perceived the government's apparent inaction to protect Germany as motivation to armed outside civil oversight. In addition, the Federal Republic's discomfort with military action after WW II was part of the reason for the extremist's self-justification.

Conversely, East Germany (German Democratic Republic, GDR) unfolded even greater efforts to militarize the population for defense preparedness. By doing so, it created worse outcomes by failing to reckon with its Nazi past. After WW II, East Germany fell into Soviet orbit as it was ruled by the Moscow-approved Socialist Unity Party

---

80 Barbara Manthe, "On the Pathway to Violence: West German Right-Wing Terrorism in the 1970s," Terrorism and Political Violence 33, no. 1 (January 2, 2021): 49–70, https://doi.org/10.1080/09546553.2018.1520701.
81 NATO's Secret Armies.

(SED). Despite claims to the contrary in propaganda, the SED accepted many former Nazis into their party and industry leadership positions with Stalin's cynicism.[82] In addition, the National Democratic Party of Germany linked up with the remaining anti-western German nationalists in the GDR.[83] One article estimates about 25 percent of the ruling SED were ex-Nazis.[84] Olaf Sundermeyer suggested that the GDR helped it's extreme right-wing thrive when it took a lackadaisical approach to its Nazi past.[85] The early SED leaders proclaimed East Germany an inherently anti-fascist state, which bore no responsibility for any Nazi past. When the armament of the new East German state advanced, and the GDR should have a paramilitary force, the SED created, trained, and equipped its Combat Groups of the Working Class along with the clandestine echelons of the regular army.[86] The combat groups operated as state-controlled militia from 1953 until 1989, like Operation Gladio's stay-behind network or the SA of former times.[87] The groups impressed citizens from the factories, agriculture cooperatives, and trade schools into light infantry/internal security training for men and medical or supply duties for women. During this time, political decisions made in East Germany created space for the future far-right to become legitimate political representation.

---

82 Vladislav M. Zubok, A Failed Empire: The Soviet Union in the Cold War from Stalin to Gorbachev, Paperback edition (Chapel Hill: University of North Carolina Press, 2009).

83 Zubok.

84 "Für Ehrliche Zusammenarbeit [For Honest Cooperation]," Der Spiegel, May 8, 1994, https://www.spiegel.de/politik/fuer-ehrliche-zusammenarbeit-a-160581e0-0002-0001-0000-000013684238.

85 Ben Knight, "The Rise of the Far-Right in the East," Deutsche Welle, September 21, 2010, https://www.dw.com/en/the-rise-of-the-far-right-in-the-east/a-5996369.

86 "NATO's Secret Armies: Chronology," Secret Warfare: Operation Gladio and NATO's Stay-Behind Armies (blog), February 2021, http://www.php.isn.ethz.ch/lory1.ethz.ch/collections/coll_gladio/chronology76c1.html?navinfo=15301.

87 Parallel History Project on Cooperative Security.

In the grey zone east of the Elbe River, East Germany's right-wing criminal gangs operated as paramilitary training groups similar to examples in the West to foment the far-right movement further. The Hengst gang was started in the GDR and covertly operated until Hengst was convicted of terrorist attacks and then expelled from East Germany. In 1971, Hengst went to West Germany to restart his outfit until Hengst was convicted of using an automatic weapon to shoot the German Communist Party office in Bonn.[88] The East German far-right movement grew during the 1970s and 1980s.[89] A book covering right-wing extremism during the period stated neo-Nazis had a hooligan or rioter classification due to East Germany's communist nomenclature idiosyncrasies, so Nazi threats were considered officially eradicated.[90] Braunthal's work describes other far-right elements in East Germany, such as anti-Semitic vandalism.[91] In other instances, Braunthal showed harassment of workers from fellow socialist countries. These attacks happened when migrants had a perception as fraternizing with East German women or compounding shortages of coveted consumer goods.[92] In the late 1980s, a compendium on German politics stated far-right groups like the Free Workers Party and the National Front formed under Stasi surveillance, GDR's equivalent of the KGB, but

88 Hans-Deitrich Genscher, "1971 Bundesamt für Verfassungsschutz Verfassungsschutzbericht [Constitutional Protection Report 1971]," accessed April 30, 2021, https://verfassungsschutzberichte.de/bund/1971?
89 Robin Ostow, "Ne Art Bürgerwehr in Form von Skins [NE Kind of Vigilante Group in the Form of Skins]: Young Germans on the Streets in the Eastern and Western States of the Federal Republic," New German Critique, no. 64 (1995): 87–103.
90 Richard Stöss, Rechtsextremismus im vereinten Deutschland [Right-Wing Extremism in United Germany], 2. unveränderte Aufl edition (Bonn: Friedrich-Ebert-Stiftung, Abteilung Dialog Ostdeutschland, 1999).
91 Braunthal, Right-Wing Extremism in Contemporary Germany.
92 Braunthal.

did little about it.[93] Finally, the Berlin Wall's fall afforded GDR's home-grown right-wing movement a new opportunity to collaborate with West German right-wing groups. The East German case shows similarities with West Germany despite its being a one-party socialist state. The paramilitaries were under state control, where they learned martial skills and applied them on the state's behalf. It is essential to recognize a continuity of pathological paramilitarism in East Germany that resemblances West Germany's case in the same period despite a heavy-handed attempt at socialist indoctrination in the East. East Germany will later become the epicenter for the populist-right AfD party suggesting a failure of the East German state to set the conditions to mitigate the far-right in modern times.

B.   MAJOR EVENTS SINCE 2014

The 2014–2015 timeframe was another cataclysm for European stability. It provided an impetus for paramilitary expansion in Germany, which policymakers were unprepared. In November 2013, the Crimean episode began with Euromaidan protests when the Russian-friendly President of Ukraine, Victor Yanukovych, would not ratify the Ukraine-European Union association agreement.[94] The agreement would bring Ukraine closer to Europe and reduce Russian influence. There were also military implications as Ukraine's control of the Sevastopol naval station meant a potential eviction of Russia's Black Sea Fleet. Pro-Ukrainian protests led to revolution and unrest.[95] The

---

93 "Handwörterbuch des politischen Systems der Bundesrepublik Deutschland [Concise Dictionary of the Political System of the Federal Republic of Germany]," in Bundeszentrale für Politische Blidung (Bundeszentrale für politische Bildung, 2021), https://www.bpb.de/nachschlagen/lexika/handwoerterbuch-politisches-system/.
94 Adrian Croft, "European Union Signs Landmark Association Agreement with Ukraine," Reuters, March 21, 2014, https://www.reuters.com/article/us-ukraine-crisis-eu-agreement-idUSBREA2K0JY20140321.
95 Mike Eckel, "A Cry from Crimea," World Policy Journal 31, no. 4 (2014): 85–96.

Russian-Crimean intervention followed in February 2014.[96] Russian separatist militias formed in Crimea amid the standoff between Ukrainian law enforcement and Russian demonstrators. At that point the little green men (Russian forces) seized roads to Sevastopol and other strategic objectives on the peninsula.[97] On 18 March 2014, Russian Crimea held a referendum, and Russian annexation went into effect.[98] The annexation allowed mobilization of separatists in the Ukrainian Donbas region, where hybrid warfare continued to destabilize the region and present a veiled threat to other European states. But the European political turmoil would not subside after the invasion due to the migrant crisis beginning months afterward.

In 2015, Angela Merkel promoted an open-door policy for those fleeing war-torn Syria, Iraq, and Afghanistan, bringing a mass wave of migration into Central Europe.[99] Millions of migrants traveled to Europe via the Mediterranean and Balkan routes.[100] The surge of migrants exceeded government capacity to humanely care for the migrants at refugee centers, so migrant camps formed along the main

---

96 Ted Poe, "Congressional Record on the Russian Invasion of Crimea," Pub. L. No. 163 Cong Rec H 2091, H2091 (2017), https://congressional-proquest-com.libproxy.nps.edu/congressional/result/congressional/congdocumentview?accountid=12702&groupid=100340&parmId=1793369AAF1.

97 Aleksandar Vasovic and Maria Kiselyova, "Russian Forces Seize Two Ukrainian Bases in Crimea," Reuters, March 19, 2014, https://www.reuters.com/article/us-ukraine-crisis-idUSBREA2I0TR20140319.

98 Steven Pifer, "Five Years after Crimea's Illegal Annexation, the Issue Is No Closer to Resolution," Brookings (blog), March 18, 2019, https://www.brookings.edu/blog/order-from-chaos/2019/03/18/five-years-after-crimeas-illegal-annexation-the-issue-is-no-closer-to-resolution/.

99 Mara Bierbach, "AfD, CDU, SPD: Where Do German Parties Stand on Refugees, Asylum and Immigration?," Deutsche Welle, September 24, 2017, https://www.dw.com/en/afd-cdu-spd-where-do-german-parties-stand-on-refugees-asylum-and-immigration/a-40610988.

100 Stefan Trines, "The State of Refugee Integration in Germany in 2019," World Education News and Reviews, August 8, 2019, https://wenr.wes.org/2019/08/the-state-of-refugee-integration-in-germany-in-2019.

thoroughfares to Northern and Central Europe.[101] Europe witnessed a coincidental increase in Islamic terrorist attacks that same year, notably in Paris, that prompted public outcry to secure Southern European borders with Turkish cooperation. Polling also showed Europeans were concerned about the migration crisis as a source of Islamic terrorism after the 2015 terror attacks.[102] The following is an infographic showing the sources and destinations of migrants in Europe.

The story of 2014–2015 was volatile and threatening to traditional European security. The Russian invasion of Crimea and Donbas justified protective, nationalistic sentiments among the right and particularly empowered the neo-Nazi affiliated extremists. The 2015 migration crisis challenged the cosmopolitan, democratic values in Germany. Germany's governing coalition misgauged public sentiment regarding migrant acceptance that ultimately put wind into the populist right's sails.

---

101 Angelique Chrisafis, Peter Walker, and Ben Quinn, "Calais 'Jungle' Camp: Clashes as Authorities Demolish Homes," Guardian, March 7, 2016, https://web.archive.org/web/20160307205334/http://www.theguardian.com/world/2016/feb/29/french-authorities-begin-clearance-of-part-of-calais-jungle-camp.
102 "European Opinions of the Refugee Crisis in 5 Charts," Pew Research Center (blog), accessed June 1, 2021, https://www.pewresearch.org/fact-tank/2016/09/16/european-opinions-of-the-refugee-crisis-in-5-charts/.

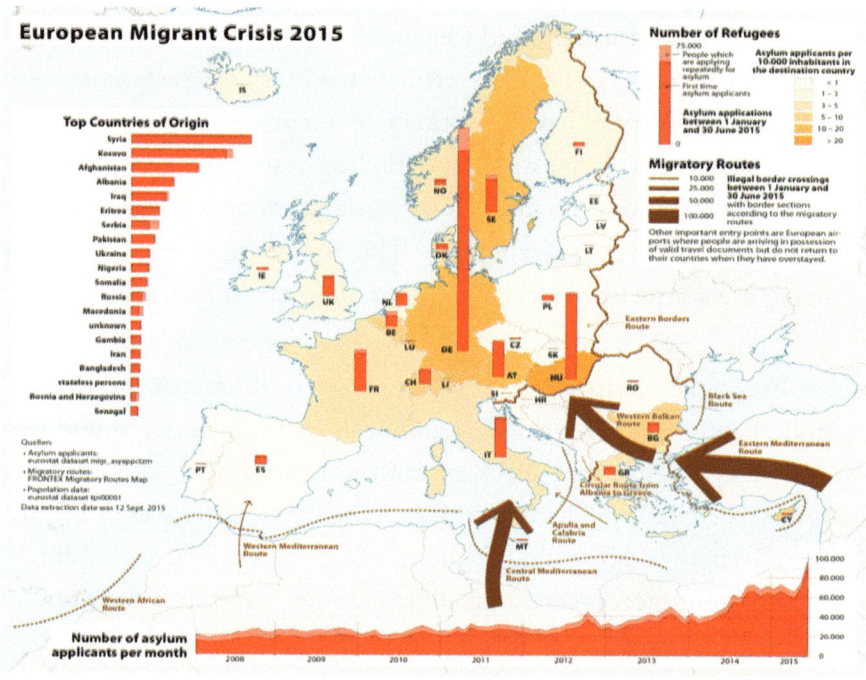

Figure 1.   European Map of Migrant Crisis 2015.[103]

C.   GERMAN RIGHT-WING LANDSCAPE

The inception of the Alternative for Germany coincided with nationalistic growth across Europe. AfD's ideals were dangerous for sustained democratic growth amongst the young, politically inexperienced Germans. AfD was also the latest Nazi-inspired political iteration. According to Jeffrey Arroyo, the party originated in 2013 with some intellectuals disappointed in Germany's bailout of Greek insolvency after the 2008 financial crisis.[104] The members put their griev-

103 Source: Maximillian Dörrbrecker, "European Migrant Crisis," in Wikipedia, October 1, 2021, https://en.wikipedia.org/w/index.php?title=European_migrant_crisis&oldid=1047564505.
104 Arroyo, Jeffrey W. AFD'S Rise: The Historical Significance And Impact On German Politics. Monterey, CA; Naval Postgraduate School, 2018.

ances into a manifesto protesting German monetary policy, which allowed unchecked financial resources into less fiscally conservative EU states. After 2013, the party worked to expand its appeal in other areas like nationalism and immigration. Although nationalistic appeals are not unprecedented in recent political usage, they are taboo and linked to far-right organizations like PEGIDA (Patriotic Europeans against Islamicisation of the West).[105] AfD politicians stated, "It's about us, our culture, our home, our Germany."[106] There was a striking similarity between AfD's statements and a Nazi slogan; "One people, one realm... "[107] Polling years after the 2014 migration crisis found Germans were still most concerned about immigration.[108] In 2017, the migrant crisis resonated with enough voters for the formerly fringe AfD party to enter parliament. Furthermore, the pro-immigration policies of the established German parties failed to allow voters opposition to migration inflow. The center-right CDU made a top-down pro-immigration decision, and in essence, a breakdown of politics occurred without differing immigration policies to choose from among those parties.

AfD continued to grow at the expense of established parties. In 2019, the AfD drew away seats from Angela Merkel's CDU in East Germany.[109] Merkel had to limit migrants to preserve her governing

105 Arroyo. AFD'S Rise: The Historical Significance And Impact On German Politics.

106 Holly Ellyatt, "Germany's Far-Right AfD Party: 5 Things You Need to Know," CNBC, September 25, 2017, https://www.cnbc.com/2017/09/25/germany-far-right-afd-party-5-things-you-need-to-know.html.

107 Joseph W. Bendersky, A Concise History of Nazi Germany, Fourth edition (Lanham: Rowman & Littlefield Publishers, 2013).

108 "A Majority of Europe's Voters Do Not Consider Migration to Be the Most Important Issue, According to Major New Poll," European Council on Foreign Relations (blog), April 1, 2019, https://ecfr.eu/article/european_voters_do_not_consider_migration_most_important_election/.

109 BBC News, "The Right-Wing Nationalists Shaking Up Europe."

coalition.[110] In 2020, AfD began to call for bans on mosque minarets and public burqa while focusing misanthropy toward the now sizable immigrant population of 21 million.[111] In 2021, AfD became the third-largest party in the Bundestag despite its *Flügel* (Wing) neo-Nazi extremism investigation.[112] But, Chancellor Merkel's stance of Germany as a welcoming country to immigrants helped AfD draw distinctions and make political gains at the CDU's expense. In this role, AfD joined a European milieu along with Poland's Law and Justice Party or Hungary's Fidesz Party, who demonstrated strong illiberal behaviors. Law and Justice and Fidesz have cracked down on media, restricted civil liberties, and prioritized the dominant ethnic group over others. More importantly, these parties provide the rhetoric for nationalism, which supports more extreme members in society as they militarize.[113] In effect, a more powerful AfD is on a trajectory to be a Nazi-adjacent actor in German politics.

The AfD's rhetoric found audiences the state strains to contain in its security services. The bizarre and unfalsifiable logic of the extremist-right makes it a cat-and-mouse game to debunk in the public forum that includes its military and security members. In addition, those who would use physical violence to protect the German homeland trend toward conservatism. Military and security members are a natural audi-

---

110 "Merkel Agrees 'Refugee Cap' in Concession to Allies," TRT World, October 9, 2017, sec. News, https://www.trtworld.com/europe/merkel-agrees-refugee-cap-in-concession-to-allies-11191.

111 "German Population of Migrant Background Rises to 21 Million," Deutsche Welle, July 28, 2020, https://www.dw.com/en/german-population-of-migrant-background-rises-to-21-million/a-54356773.

112 "Germany Places Entire Far-Right AfD Under Surveillance," Deutsche Welle, March 3, 2021, https://www.dw.com/en/germany-places-entire-far-right-afd-under-surveillance-reports/a-56757489.

113 Bieber, "How Europe's Nationalists Became Internationalists."

ence, perhaps even target, for the populist right's rhetoric. The line between German conservatism and pathology is critically important for civilian authorities to define.

However, the conversation started in society. Political entities such as AfD, The III. (pronounced the Third Way), and *Die Rechte* (The Right) operated publicly but have overlapping membership with many hardcore extremists.[114] These groups included *Reichsbürger* who are citizens refusing the modern German state's political authority and geographic boundaries in favor of an imagined still-existent 1937 German state. The *Wutbürger* were enraged citizens who felt the German government was making decisions outside of democratic control, while the doomsday-prepper movement had an apocalyptic outlook. Some groups like the Reichsbürger became more martial as they prepared for "Day X," which is a forthcoming violent coup against the German government. A more recent incarnation was the *Querdenker* movement.[115] The Querdenker community's central effort was protesting Covid-19 restrictions and was analogous to the American QAnon community. These movements are more or less interchangeable as a vehicle for far-right activity. The following is a picture from 2019 right-wing demonstration against Angela Merkel.

114 Braunthal, G. 2009. Right-Wing Extremism in Contemporary Germany. 1st ed. 2009. London: Palgrave Macmillan UK. https://doi.org/10.1057/9780230251168.
115 Mercel Fürstenau, "Meet Germany's 'Querdenker' COVID Protest Movement," Deutsche Welle, March 4, 2021, https://www.dw.com/en/meet-germanys-querdenker-covid-protest-movement/a-57049985.

Figure 2.   A 2019 *Wir für Deutschland* protest in Berlin.[116]

Germany's Basic Law made it impossible for overt neo-Nazis to display sig runes or make Hitler salute at rallies. Instead, the modern German extreme-right used cryptic demonstrations around peripheral issues in physical space. Protests against Covid restrictions became a valuable gathering opportunity for these various groups with latent anti-democratic principles. The premise was to erode trust in government institutions. The threat is two-fold. On the one hand, right-wing extremism questions European federalism through the AfD as a polit-

116 Leonhard Lenz, Demonstration von Wir Für Deutschland Am 3. Oktober 2019 in Berlin [Demonstration by Wir Für Deutschland on October 3, 2019 in Berlin], October 3, 2019, October 3, 2019, Own work, https://commons.wiki-media.org/wiki/File:Demonstration_of_Wir_f%C3%BCr_Deutschland_2019-10-03_15.jpg.

ical vehicle. A united Europe within the EU and NATO stop a centuries-long cycle of economic and military competition between states. On the other, Russia remains a threat to integration. Russia is willing to exploit the far-right's Euroscepticism or reaction to the migration crisis to train a virulent right-wing paramilitarism the Federal government must attend. Russia is the ultimate benefactor of both problems.

The inception of the Alternative for Germany coincided with nationalistic growth across Europe. AfD's ideals were dangerous for sustained democratic growth amongst the young, politically inexperienced Germans. AfD was also the latest Nazi-inspired political iteration. According to Jeffrey Arroyo, the party originated in 2013 with some intellectuals disappointed in Germany's bailout of Greek insolvency after the 2008 financial crisis.[117] The members put their grievances into a manifesto protesting German monetary policy, which allowed unchecked financial resources into less fiscally conservative EU states. After 2013, the party worked to expand its appeal in other areas like nationalism and immigration. Although nationalistic appeals are not unprecedented in recent political usage, they are taboo and linked to far-right organizations like PEGIDA (Patriotic Europeans against Islamicisation of the West).[118] AfD politicians stated, "It's about us, our culture, our home, our Germany."[119] There was a striking similarity between AfD's statements and a Nazi slogan; "One people, one realm... "[120] Polling years after the 2014 migration crisis found Germans were

117 Arroyo, Jeffrey W. AFD'S Rise: The Historical Significance And Impact On German Politics. Monterey, CA; Naval Postgraduate School, 2018.
118 Arroyo. AFD'S Rise: The Historical Significance And Impact On German Politics.
119 Holly Ellyatt, "Germany's Far-Right AfD Party: 5 Things You Need to Know," CNBC, September 25, 2017, https://www.cnbc.com/2017/09/25/germany-far-right-afd-party-5-things-you-need-to-know.html.
120 Joseph W. Bendersky, A Concise History of Nazi Germany, Fourth edition (Lanham: Rowman & Littlefield Publishers, 2013).

still most concerned about immigration.[121] In 2017, the migrant crisis resonated with enough voters for the formerly fringe AfD party to enter parliament. Furthermore, the pro-immigration policies of the established German parties failed to allow voters opposition to migration inflow. The center-right CDU made a top-down pro-immigration decision, and in essence, a breakdown of politics occurred without differing immigration policies to choose from among those parties.

AfD continued to grow at the expense of established parties. In 2019, the AfD drew away seats from Angela Merkel's CDU in East Germany.[122] Merkel had to limit migrants to preserve her governing coalition.[123] In 2020, AfD began to call for bans on mosque minarets and public burqa while focusing misanthropy toward the now sizable immigrant population of 21 million.[124] In 2021, AfD became the third-largest party in the Bundestag despite its *Flügel* (Wing) neo-Nazi extremism investigation.[125] But, Chancellor Merkel's stance of Germany as a welcoming country to immigrants helped AfD draw distinctions and make political gains at the CDU's expense. In this role, AfD joined a European milieu along with Poland's Law and Justice Party or Hungary's Fidesz Party, who demonstrated strong illiberal behaviors. Law and Justice and Fidesz have cracked down on media, restricted civil

---

121 "A Majority of Europe's Voters Do Not Consider Migration to Be the Most Important Issue, According to Major New Poll," European Council on Foreign Relations (blog), April 1, 2019, https://ecfr.eu/article/european_voters_do_not_consider_migration_most_important_election/.

122 BBC News, "The Right-Wing Nationalists Shaking Up Europe."

123 "Merkel Agrees 'Refugee Cap' in Concession to Allies," TRT World, October 9, 2017, sec. News, https://www.trtworld.com/europe/merkel-agrees-refugee-cap-in-concession-to-allies-11191.

124 "German Population of Migrant Background Rises to 21 Million," Deutsche Welle, July 28, 2020, https://www.dw.com/en/german-population-of-migrant-background-rises-to-21-million/a-54356773.

125 "Germany Places Entire Far-Right AfD Under Surveillance," Deutsche Welle, March 3, 2021, https://www.dw.com/en/germany-places-entire-far-right-afd-under-surveillance-reports/a-56757489.

liberties, and prioritized the dominant ethnic group over others. More importantly, these parties provide the rhetoric for nationalism, which supports more extreme members in society as they militarize.[126] In effect, a more powerful AfD is on a trajectory to be a Nazi-adjacent actor in German politics.

The AfD's rhetoric found audiences the state strains to contain in its security services. The bizarre and unfalsifiable logic of the extremist-right makes it a cat-and-mouse game to debunk in the public forum that includes its military and security members. In addition, those who would use physical violence to protect the German homeland trend toward conservatism. Military and security members are a natural audience, perhaps even target, for the populist right's rhetoric. The line between German conservatism and pathology is critically important for civilian authorities to define.

However, the conversation started in society. Political entities such as AfD, The III. (pronounced the Third Way), and *Die Rechte* (The Right) operated publicly but have overlapping membership with many hardcore extremists.[127] These groups included *Reichsbürger* who are citizens refusing the modern German state's political authority and geographic boundaries in favor of an imagined still-existent 1937 German state. The *Wutbürger* were enraged citizens who felt the German government was making decisions outside of democratic control, while the doomsday-prepper movement had an apocalyptic outlook. Some groups like the Reichsbürger became more martial as they prepared for "Day X," which is a forthcoming violent coup against the German government. A more recent incarnation was the *Querdenker* movement.[128]

126 Bieber, "How Europe's Nationalists Became Internationalists."
127 Braunthal, G. 2009. Right-Wing Extremism in Contemporary Germany. 1st ed. 2009. London: Palgrave Macmillan UK. https://doi.org/10.1057/9780230251168.
128 Mercel Fürstenau, "Meet Germany's 'Querdenker' COVID Protest Movement," Deutsche Welle, March 4, 2021, https://www.dw.com/en/meet-germanys-querdenker-covid-protest-movement/a-57049985.

The Querdenker community's central effort was protesting Covid-19 restrictions and was analogous to the American QAnon community. These movements are more or less interchangeable as a vehicle for far-right activity. The following is a picture from 2019 right-wing demonstration against Angela Merkel.

Germany's Basic Law made it impossible for overt neo-Nazis to display sig runes or make Hitler salute at rallies. Instead, the modern German extreme-right used cryptic demonstrations around peripheral issues in physical space. Protests against Covid restrictions became a valuable gathering opportunity for these various groups with latent anti-democratic principles. The premise was to erode trust in government institutions. The threat is two-fold. On the one hand, right-wing extremism questions European federalism through the AfD as a political vehicle. A united Europe within the EU and NATO stop a centuries-long cycle of economic and military competition between states. On the other, Russia remains a threat to integration. Russia is willing to exploit the far-right's Euroscepticism or reaction to the migration crisis to train a virulent right-wing paramilitarism the Federal government must attend. Russia is the ultimate benefactor of both problems.

D.   GERMAN PARAMILITARIES

Germany's paramilitary scene was an underground phenomenon accompanied by growth in problematic areas. There was an apparent growth in paramilitary activity, which the civil-military structure must address and thus far have mostly failed to find answers to the problem.[129] Coinciding with the regional instability was a migration cri-

---

129 Donald Abenheim, Carolyn Halladay, and Rachel Epstein, "Radicalization in the German Armed Forces and Beyond," Political Violence at a Glance, May 7, 2019, https://politicalviolenceataglance.org/2019/05/07/radicalization-in-the-german-armed-forces-and-beyond/.

sis, an uptick in populist-right parties throughout Europe, and an increase in paramilitary activity. Nationalism and history have resurfaced to guide the paramilitary cadre into new zeal with action in conflict zones. A Soufan Center report suggested up to 165 German paramilitarists fought in Ukraine between 2014 and 2019.[130] An International Centre for Counter-Terrorism report sponsored by the Dutch government estimated that between 720 and 760 Germans were active in Iraq and Syrian conflict zones.[131] Domestically, the far-right scene feeding into paramilitarism appeared to be on the rise, especially in the East, as neo-Nazi gangs attacked foreigners and provided AfD's most significant support.[132] It also suggested that these individuals would be susceptible to further extremism.

German government investigations have found elements of the extreme right in its defense apparatus. The Franco Albrecht affair stood out in this connection, according to an interview with German extremism researchers Carolyn Halladay and Donald Abenheim.[133] Albrecht gravitated to the most extreme elements within the German government. Albrecht entered the Bundeswehr officer candidate program, where he wrote a thesis on *völkish* (Germanic ethno-nationalist) ideology.[134] With his thesis rejected for racist views, the Bundeswehr became suspicious of his character, but the Bundeswehr Disciplinary Authority

---

130 Jason Blazakis et al., "White Supremacy Extremism: The Transnational Rise of the Violent White Supremacist Movement" (The Soufan Center, September), https://thesoufancenter.org/research/white-supremacy-extremism-the-transnational-rise-of-the-violent-white-supremacist-movement/.
131 Bibi van Ginkel et al., "The Foreign Fighters Phenomenon in the European Union. Profiles, Threats & Policies," ed. Eva Entenmann, Terrorism and Counter-Terrorism Studies, April 1, 2016, https://doi.org/10.19165/2016.1.02.
132 Denijal Jegic, "How East Germany Became a Stronghold of the Far Right," accessed April 19, 2021, https://www.aljazeera.com/opinions/2018/9/29/how-east-germany-became-a-stronghold-of-the-far-right.
133 Abenheim, Halladay, and Epstein, "Radicalization in the German Armed Forces and Beyond."
134 Abenheim, Halladay, and Epstein.

relented. He commissioned as a lieutenant and went on to find common ground with other right-wing extremists in the Bundeswehr and *Kommando Spezialkräfte* (KSK) as a covert coup organizer. In 2016, Albrecht began planning the paramilitary Uniter network consisting of police, soldiers, and members of the constitutional protection office. The Uniter network was suspected to be planning attacks on prominent members of government who facilitated the refugee throughput into Germany, such as President Joachim Gauck, Minister of Justice Heiko Maas, and Green Party politician Claudia Roth.[135] Uniter even had insignia patches made to signify friend from foe on Day X. Albrecht's Uniter network merged with the like-minded putsch-oriented Hannibal network in the German KSK.

Albrecht's plot lead to a national controversy. In February 2017, Albrecht was arrested for attempting to smuggle a pistol into an airport in Vienna. His case remains the stuff of tabloids as court rulings continue as of 2021. Arguably, his deep connections into the defense apparatus's far-right extremism and targeting of democratically elected politicians could be considered more problematic. In 2020, Kassel council president Walter Lübcke was murdered for his pro-migration stance by a man authorities suspect was connected to the National Socialist Underground.[136] The paramilitarists must coexist with the military partly due to an affinity for military service and partly for the need for weapons training the military provides. In some ways, Germany's

135 Sebastian Erb, "Rechtsextreme Netzwerke in Deutschland: Ein deutscher Soldat [Right-Wing Extremist Networks in Germany: A German Soldier]," Die Tageszeitung, May 16, 2021, sec. taz, society, https://taz.de/!5767295/.
136 "New Twist in Case of Slain German Politician Walter Lübcke," Deutsche Welle, September 1, 2020, https://www.dw.com/en/new-twist-in-case-of-slain-german-politician-walter-l%C3%BCbcke/a-51935858.

strict gun control facilitates exposure to extremism within the military.[137] The Albrecht affair and Lübke's death demonstrate violent intent among some on the German far-right.

The Albrecht affair showed one troubling aspect of extremism, but there were more. Some paramilitaries without military connections trained in *Partizan* camps near St. Petersburg, Russia.[138] These camps attracted right-wing members of III. and those militarized in ideology. The course was a week of focused study on paramilitary skills like marksmanship, triage, wilderness survival, psyops, mine laying in tandem with improvised-explosive training.[139] Russian combat veterans operated the location with links to the neo-Nazi Russian Imperial Movement (RIM) as well as some suspected assistance from Russia's Ministry of Defense. The U.S. State Department classified RIM as a terrorist organization. The German government cannot stop its citizens from training in Partizan camps, so it remained a boon for the German paramilitary movement. These examples show the trend of a changing face of paramilitarism in Central Europe. The modern paramilitaries are a severe threat to democracy due to their proliferation within and without the government structure. They show a capacity to evade detective agencies within the government while they spread the message through the German defense apparatus. It is also problematic as Germany is the cornerstone of the European project. If paramilitaries can undermine Germany from within, Europe becomes more chaotic and volatile to the world's detriment.

---

137 Edith Palmer, "Firearms-Control Legislation and Policy: Germany," Web page, Law Library of Congress, accessed April 19, 2021,
https://www.loc.gov/law/help/firearms-control/germany.php.
138 Robert Lansing Institute, "Combat Training for European Neo-Nazis in Russia," Robert Lansing Institute (blog), June 9, 2020, https://lansinginstitute.org/2020/06/09/combat-training-for-european-neo-nazis-in-russia/.
139 Robert Lansing Institute.

German news articles covered several other extremist instances in the German military. In one article series by Deutsche Welle covering German military extremism, 2019 had 360 Bundeswehr extremism cases, but by 2020, German Military Counterintelligence Services (*Militärische Abschirmdienst*, MAD) started 500 extremist investigations in the Bundeswehr.[140] In 2021, two Bundeswehr reservists ceased participation due to extremist allegations after an internal audit.[141] The chairman of the Bielefeld reservist unit was suspected when a social media post showed him at a Querdenker protest in a neo-Nazi supporting sweater. He had to end his membership when the Berlin contingent of reservists became aware and reported the post to the Bundeswehr. Then there are the problems with the special forces' unit KSK. The KSK is Germany's highly secretive special operations branch of the Bundeswehr. A KSK unit with unauthorized weapons and Nazi paraphernalia hidden by some soldiers was exposed. In another instance, 48,000 rounds of small-arm ammunition and 62 kilograms of explosives had gone missing.[142] The MAD suspected 20 individuals of wrongdoing. These situations led to Defense Minister Annegret Kramp-Kerrenbauer standing down a unit of approximately a quarter of the KSK's size in

---

140 Christina Burack, "Germany: Over 500 Right-Wing Extremists Suspected in Bundeswehr," Deutsche Welle, January 26, 2020, https://www.dw.com/en/germany-over-500-right-wing-extremists-suspected-in-bundeswehr/a-52152558.
141 "Bielefelder Rechtsextreme unterwandern Reservisten der Bundeswehr [Bielefeld Right-Wing Extremists Infiltrate Bundeswehr Reservists]," Neue Westfälische, May 2, 2021, https://www.nw.de/lokal/bielefeld/mitte/22948818_Bielefelder-Rechtsextreme-unterwandern-Reservisten-der-Bundeswehr.html.
142 "'Toxic Leadership Culture': Germany Shakes Up Elite Army Force Over Far-Right Links," Local Germany, June 30, 2020, https://www.thelocal.de/20200630/germany-to-partly-dissolve-elite-force-over-far-right-links-minister/.

June 2020 due to a toxic leadership structure.[143] There was further concern that the unit had become partially independent of democratic control.[144] Minister Kramp-Kerrenbauer scrutinized the head of MAD, Christof Gramm, for the situation in the German military. Gramm's remediation appeared insufficient and lost his job in September of 2020.[145] Examples of German extremism are plentiful during the late 2010s period.

These examples from Albrecht to Gramm lead some to consider the possibility of a shadow army within the Bundeswehr. More covert groups are not a remote possibility. The ideologues in government structure are a major problem for the German state because Russian can exploit them using hybrid warfare strategies. German government as a sanctuary for the far-right means it cannot combat the paramilitary or militant extremist problems as required. Democratic control of the military is decreased, and public confidence is eroded. The phenomenon helps the illiberal populists call for strongmen to solve the problems, which is a hard-learned lesson for Germany.

E.   GERMAN RESPONSE TO PARAMILITARISM

The German state response is not a policy gap; instead, there is a security issue where policy meets loose enforcement, blind eyes, or sympathetic administrators. The right-wing problem in government is encouraged through negligence. Right-wing extremism in government

---

143 Katrin Bennhold, "As Neo-Nazis Seed Military Ranks, Germany Confronts 'an Enemy Within' - The New York Times," New York Times, July 3, 2020, https://www.nytimes.com/2020/07/03/world/europe/germany-military-neo-nazis-ksk.html.
144 Local, "'Toxic Leadership Culture.'"
145 "Germany Replaces Military Intelligence Boss after Far-Right Scandals," Reuters, September 24, 2020, https://www.reuters.com/article/us-germany-military-farright-idUSKCN26F2ZJ.

handled by elected officials at the highest echelon of government suggests subordinates do not agree or do not care about civilian policy regarding acceptable standards for military behavior. The German government's response to its paramilitaries and right-wing extremism starts with its policy documents and security institutions.

Domestically, right-wing extremism is the operating handle set by German authority. Tactically, domestic terrorism falls to *GSG9 Der Bundespolizei* (Federal Police) and is analogous to the U.S. SWAT teams. But GSG9 has its problems with Nazi inspiration when its former head, Ulrich Wegener, and former KSK head, Reinhard Günzel, authoring a book praising their respective unit's historical connection to the elite Wehrmacht Brandenburger unit.[146] The Brandenburger connection to their units is not unreasonable, but it is not reassuring either. Germany has a Joint Terrorism and Extremism Prevention Center (*Gemeinsames Extremismus und Terrorismusabwehr-Zentrum*, GETZ) to coordinate its 40 security agencies to prevent and combat politically motivated violence and subversion.[147] Constitutionally, the ultimate authority is the Federal Office for the Protection of the Constitution (*Bundesamt für Verfassungsschutz*, BfV).[148] BfV is an early warning system for democracy. According to the Counter Extremism Project, the BfV has a list of 32,000 individuals tracked for far-right activity, with propaganda offenses being the

146 "Verbrecher Als Vorbilder? [Criminals as Role Models?]," Der Spiegel, February 25, 2007, https://www.spiegel.de/politik/verbrecher-als-vorbilder-a-e7cdec37-0002-0001-0000-000050666658.
147 Federal Criminal Police Office, "BKA - Joint Extremism and Terrorism Defense Center (GETZ)," accessed May 31, 2021, https://www.bka.de/DE/UnsereAufgaben/Kooperationen/GETZ/getz_node.html.
148 Federal Office for the Protection of the Constitution, "Rechtsextremismus [Right-Wing Extremism]," Bundesamt für Verfassungsschutz, accessed May 31, 2021, http://www.verfassungsschutz.de/DE/themen/rechtsextremismus/rechtsextremismus_node.html.

most common indictment.[149] BfV monitors the AfD party in Thuringia and Saxony-Anhalt for constitutional violations.[150] Militarily, the MAD is the central constitutional protective agency within the defense apparatus, analogous to NCIS.[151] Germany retains a credible and effective anti-terrorism capability.

As far as Russia underwriting German militant extremism, a *2016 White Paper* on German Security Policy states the world is unsettled and "peace and stability are not a matter of course."[152] That suggests Germany is aware of Russia as a threat, but Germany still might not have plans to respond to Russia and hybrid war. The White Paper acknowledges paramilitaries in relation to hybrid warfare. Russia's hybrid warfare uses all possible means below the provocation needed to justify military retaliation but is meant to undermine and compromise the target state. The report states a need for analytical capability and an early-warning system to identify the threat. Furthermore, prevention is a whole-of-society response to these irregular elements. German security is also reliant on NATO and a coherent EU, so these sources might bolster German security if prioritization is on hybrid war and paramilitarism.

The last *White Paper* is from 2016, so one must assume the Federal Republic is renovating its emphasis to counter the problems in security. A 2018 German defense working paper suggests a continuance

---

149 Counter Extremism Project, "Germany: Extremism and Terrorism" (Counter Extremism Project, May 2021), https://www.counterextremism.com/countries/germany.
150 Counter Extremism Project.
151 MAD, "Der Militärische Abschirmdienst [The Military Counterintelligence]," accessed May 31, 2021, https://www.bundeswehr.de/de/organisation/weitere-bmvg-dienststellen/mad-bundesamt-fuer-den-militaerischen-abschirmdienst.
152 2016 White Paper On German Security Policy and the Future of the Bundeswehr (Berlin: Federal Ministry of Defense, 2016), https://issat.dcaf.ch/download/111704/2027268/2016%20White%20Paper.pdf.

of the whole-of-government strategy.[153] It recognizes Russia as a primary threat using hybrid war where a battle is denied to NATO forces to implement lower intensity struggle such as using little green men that cannot be attributed to Russia. The document concludes with a recommendation for Germany to define what the total defense would be in the face of current hybrid threats. Germany takes further action on paramilitarism through an amended Nationality Act, which revoked dual citizens' German nationality if discovered as a terrorist combatant.[154] The amendment also hires hundreds more investigators, but these enforcement efforts do not apply to retroactive cases, so it falls short for practical purposes. Germany is increasing its military spending to reach 2 percent of GDP NATO.[155] In context, Germany has not allocated this much funding to its military since 1988 but is doing so after the 2014 Wales NATO summit where hybrid warfare enters the conversation.

The example of the German state response is troubling because Europe's economic and potential military powerhouse is struggling to contain the extremism threat. Pairing the problem with Turkey's ability to weaponize migration, and Russia's exploitation of right-wing movement means Germany requires policy renovation regarding the multicausal issue.[156] The extremist right's actions are illegal. Yet, they are

---

153 Philipp Lange, "Total Defence: How Germany Should Implement A Whole-of-Government National and Collective Defence" (German Federal Academy for Security Policy, January 2, 2018), https://www.baks.bund.de/en/working-papers/2018/total-defence-how-germany-should-implement-a-whole-of-government-national-and.

154 "Country Reports on Terrorism 2019: Germany," United States Department of State, May 31, 2021, https://www.state.gov/reports/country-reports-on-terrorism-2019/germany/.

155 Daniel Heinrich, "SIPRI: Germany Significantly Increases Military Spending," Deutsche Welle, April 26, 2020, https://www.dw.com/en/sipri-germany-significantly-increases-military-spending/a-53250926.

156 "Migrant Crisis: Russia and Syria 'Weaponising' Migration," BBC News, March 2, 2016, https://www.bbc.com/news/world-europe-35706238.

flourishing in the Bundeswehr, KSK, and even amongst civil servants meant to warn of their presence. Germany's problems go beyond the civil-military dynamic as conventionally understood to include the fabric of German society, which Russia empowers Germany's far-right to destroy.

F.   DISCUSSION

History serves as a prologue for the future in the minds of the paramilitary members. Germany's Nazi specter empowers those right-wing groups looking to the past for ideology besides rhetoric, which carries meaning in the 21st-century context. In some ways, the Nazi past is immortal in that it serves as inspiration for Pan-European nationalist groups throughout Europe and North America. The populist-right, militant right-wing extremists, and entities outside the country curate a gentrified Nazism for those exhausted with their democracy's policy on Islamic migration or their governments' perceived weakness in Europe.

Germany's Bundeswehr has been following the Janowitzian model of civil-military synchronization with citizens in uniform concepts more than Huntington's professionalization.[157] The Germans prefer intervention in military affairs, as showcased by the recent far-right military cases. But in practical terms, Janowitzian military thinking means enlisting many far-right believers from society. The nature of German defense is the NATO alliance, which is cooperative and requires pragmatist military leaders representing German strategic thought. However, the German pragmatist is unlikely to take extreme

---

157 Donald Abenheim and Carolyn Halladay, "Professional Soldiers and Citizens in Uniform: Some Thoughts on Innere Führung from a Transatlantic Perspective" (Monterey, CA, Naval Post Graduate School, 2016), https://calhoun.nps.edu/bitstream/handle/10945/57113/Abenheim_Professional_Soldiers_and_Citizens_in_Uniform.pdf?sequence=1&isAllowed=y.

action to deter, nor defeat a hybrid war scenario, latent far-right extremism, or the Crimean invasion due to their constrained outlook and the collaborative nature of the alliance prevents overreaction. Russia need only take a Russian-majority city in Estonia like Narva to completely undermine the NATO alliance and German defensive arrangements, which Germany is unprepared for.

The German case shows how Janowitz's conception of civil-military relations in some ways falls short. The AfD has connections to other Eurosceptic parties in the European Parliament Identity and Democracy (ID) bloc. The ID bloc work against many established financial and security agreements, similar to the ways Brexit cast doubts on these arrangements. The ID-aligned parties give the extremist elements a voice and some political might. Institutions looking to mitigate the right-wing's hold on paramilitary history are served by acknowledging it and developing complementary policy while implementing it much more robustly than the present.

The German government has done a poor job solving the problem, as evidenced in the popularity of the far-right in security circles, parliament, and the larger society. The active conflict zones in Ukraine pose another issue as they are a destination for paramilitary forces recruited in Germany. The defense apparatus becomes less an instrument of state policy following the civilian-democratic rationale but a security concern. There are parallels to the WW I aftermath. After WW I, the returning veterans joined the Freikorps for the opportunity to do meaningful work putting down civil unrest. German International Security Assistance Forces (ISAF) return from Iraq and Afghanistan to domestic turbulence in migration or rising populist-right sentiments, suggesting these veterans volunteer for paramilitary organizations like their WW I forefathers did.

The combined effect is that there is a viable threat to German democracy. Russia hopes to destabilize Germany further by manipulation of hybrid warfare. Russia has attempted to weaponized German history and politics to exploit the divisions within society to revise the European order. If Russia can influence Germany into a Eurosceptic dead end by feeding the dialogue of the far-right, then its hybrid strategy is successful. On the other hand, if Russia can depose Merkel in favor of a pro-Moscow SPD, that works too. These are two strategies to recreate the modern Holy Alliance with Vladimir Putin consolidating influence in East and Central Europe. Paramilitarism is central to both lines of effort: Russian revision of Central European order and European federative disintegration.

III. POLAND

The Polish paramilitary case shows a blend of problems from wider Europe and Polish society while offering prospects for their security. Polish paramilitarism is robust due to the state's near-constant occupation since the end of the Polish-Lithuanian commonwealth. The sense of nationalism in Poland as embodied by its paramilitary cadre is undeniable and unique. Like its German counterpart, Polish paramilitaries challenge aspects of the European project because they incorporate a far-right nationalism in opposition to cosmopolitanism and Western integration. Poland handled the migration crisis of 2014 in ways that opposed the European consensus. Poland essentially closed its borders to immigrants. When the Crimean invasion happened, it started weaponizing against Russian revisionism by grafting the latent paramilitary cadre into state structure.[158] However, these responses are far from perfect. With Ukraine on its border, Poland supplies its share of vigilante warriors. Russia encourages Ukrainian divisions that draw Poles into the fight to further Russian interests in Ukraine while threatening the Baltics.[159] The populist-right Law and Justice Party (*Prawo i Sprawiedliwość*, PiS), currently in power, use these fears to advance a contrarian European agenda that places the United States above the rest of the NATO alliance to Poland's ultimate detriment. Ultimately, Polish paramilitarism embodies a changing face of European nationalism from the integrationist hopes of the 1990s.

A. PARAMILITARY HISTORY

Polish paramilitarism reckons itself as the nationalistic force essential to creating the modern Polish state. Poland struggled with the

---

158 "Fala Uchodźców? Statystyki Studzą Emocje [A Wave of Refugees? Statistics Cool Down Emotions]," Polska Times, September 25, 2015, https://polskatimes.pl/fala-uchodzcow-statystyki-studza-emocje/ar/8180618.
159 NATO, "Readiness Action Plan."

surrounding empires in the partitions of the late 18th century, most notably with Russia, but it lost territory to the Austrian and Prussian empires. Polish military-aged males were in Russian service following Poland's final partition in 1795 when the Polish Kingdom collapsed.[160] Military insurrection occasionally surfaced against Tsarist Russia throughout the 19th century, and these uprisings served as a focal point for the later-realized Polish national awakening.[161] The Polish paramilitary tradition began to take its romanticized, later imitated form just before WW I. Just as in Germany, Polish paramilitarism flourished in the chaos prior to and immediately after WW I. In 1910, ZS *Strzelec* (Rifleman's Association) formed in L'viv to establish an independent republic from the Polish enclave of the Austrian empire under famed Polish commander Józef Piłsudski in exchange for their support against the Imperial Russian Army.[162] ZS Strzelec went dormant during WW I, as Piłsudski took command of the Polish Legions of the Austro-Hungarian Army.[163] Piłsudski was afforded a dominant, even authoritarian position in Poland's political sphere after the war and established an illiberal element in the new post-war Polish republic. The post-war period saw the Polish paramilitary become a dynamic force working for Polish statehood centered in Warsaw. Therefore, Polish paramilitarism preceded and was essential to the creation of the state.

The combination of independence, lawlessness, and militarism in Poland created some of the Polish paramilitary identity. The Polish Republic had new life in the aftermath of Russia's WW I defeat. The

160 Robert Bideleux and Ian Jeffries, A History of Eastern Europe: Crisis and Change, 1st edition (London ; New York: Routledge, 1998).
161 Bideleux and Jeffries.
162 Bob Tarwacki, "The Rifleman's Association: Origins and Outcomes of a Nationalistic, Polish Social Movement" (City University of New York, 2005), https://www.academia.edu/4434881/The_Riflemans_Association_Origins_and_Outcomes_of_a_Nationalistic_Polish_Social_Movement.
163 Robert Gerwarth and John Horne, War in Peace: Paramilitary Violence in Europe after the Great War, Reprint edition (Oxford: Oxford University Press, 2013).

Treaty of Versailles forced Imperial Germany to acknowledge Polish control of the corridor to the Baltic Sea near the Prussian city of Danzig.[164] The Polish functionaries used ZS Strzelec and other Polish paramilitary organizations as a startup army until the Polish state could field a conventional state-controlled army.[165] Poland then hosted the war after the war from 1918 to 1921, coinciding with continued paramilitary violence after the armistice.[166] The war after the war meant that paramilitary forces commenced ethnic cleansing in Poland's newly created borderlands where Imperial Germany and Tsarist Russia had previously existed. These paramilitaries targeted ethnic Ukrainians and Russians in eastern Poland, committed pogroms against Polish-Jews, and harassed ethnic Germans in western Poland.[167] The Polish far-right paramilitary can point to this interwar era as its origin story, emphasizing the ethnic aspect of the Polish national struggle.

Poland had several contributing factors to the interwar activity like the distrust of Russia, a mass return of war veterans, and a weak, decentralized, young Polish authority unable to intervene effectively. Soviet Russia was engulfed in civil war since 1917 and reneged on the Treaty of Brest-Litovsk mandate to respect Polish territorial integrity.[168] The Polish militia fought to secure the homeland against revolutionary Russia's western-most advances into Poland.[169] The struggle was so

---

164 William McNeill, History of Western Civilization: A Handbook (University of Chicago Press), accessed August 10, 2021, https://www.amazon.com/History-Western-Civilization-William-McNeill/dp/0226561607/ref=asc_df_0226561607/?tag=hyprod-20&linkCode=df0&hvadid=241953224058&hvpos=&hvnetw=g&hvrand=394143 4626762747878&hvpone=&hvptwo=&hvqmt=&hvdev=c&hvdvcmdl=&hvlocint =&hvlocphy=9031899&hvtargid=pla-489122852321&psc=1.
165 Gerwarth and Horne, War in Peace.
166 Peter Gartell, 'War after the War: Conflicts 1919-1923' in A Companion to World War 1, ed. John Horne (Oxford University Press, 2010), 558-75.
167 Gerwarth and Horne, War in Peace.
168 Gerwarth and Horne.
169 Gerwarth and Horne.

ubiquitous that by 1918 a female-led independence group called the Volunteer Women's Legion defended L'viv in the Polish-Ukrainian War and then in the Polish-Soviet War under Col. Aleksandra Zagórshka.[170] Also, in 1918, WW I commander Józef Piłsudski became Chief of State and then Prime Minister. A 1926 coup allowed Piłsudski to transform Poland into an authoritarian state.[171] The Polish case shows a popular nationalistic independence movement in the early 20th, century followed by paramilitaries that helped to solidify the state but contributed to much of its problems.

The WWII era continued and expanded the trend of paramilitarism in Polish society, particularly in its nascent stages where totalitarian states surrounding Poland were plotting the republic's demise with the secret Molotov-Ribbentrop pact.[172] In 1939, the Nazis and then the Soviets invaded with the Polish army caught between a dual attack. The country was then jointly occupied by Nazi Germany and the Soviet Union during WW II.

WW II represented the solidification of paramilitarism as a Polish device for independence—albeit with divergent, sometimes mutually antagonist political aims. For example, paramilitary elements composed a part of the Polish Home Army, an underground organization under the Nazi occupation. The Home Army's forest people, a guerilla subset that occupied the forests, numbered 4,000 people but harassed German units in several battles throughout the war.[173] The

---

170 Agnieszka Cieślikowa, Ochotnicza Legia Kobiet [Volunteer Legia Women]: 1918-1922 (Warszawa: Bellona, 1998), https://www.amazon.com/Ochotnicza-Legia-Kobiet-1918-1922-Polish/dp/8311088780.
171 Joseph Rothschild, Pilsudski's Coup D'etat., East Central European Studies of Columbia University (Columbia University Press, 1966).
172 Vyacheslav Molotov and Joachim von Ribbentrop, "Molotov-Ribbentrop Pact" (Fordham University, August 23, 1939), https://sourcebooks.fordham.edu/mod/1939pact.asp.
173 Roy Francis Leslie, ed., History of Poland since 1863 (Cambridge ; New York: Cambridge University Press, 1983).

Peasants' Battalions were a larger paramilitary at about 160,000 people who sabotaged and murdered to deter German collaborators in Poland.[174] Yet another group was the Polish Workers Army, with 20,000 participants acting during the German retreat. The Polish Workers Army represented the armed underground socialist movement; its members were just as likely to fight and sabotage other Polish resistance groups as their Nazi occupiers.[175] Conversely, the National Armed Forces fought alongside the Nazis against the Red Army and their socialist partisans.[176] Meanwhile, Poland's exiled-in-London army sent troops to allied military forces, notably in Italy, and into the Red Army.[177] The various Polish paramilitaries during WW II fought in some dire conditions that solidified their willingness to fight Europe's greatest armies.

The state to emerge from the war was the Peoples' Republic of Poland (*Polska Rzeczpospolita*), which controlled the Polish military, paramilitary or otherwise. Poland then disbanded ZS Strzelec and the Home Army in favor of state-controlled paramilitaries like Citizens' Militia and the more rudimentary Volunteer Reserve of Citizens Militia

---

174 Bogumił Karaszewski, Partyzancka broń: O uzbrojeniu w Batalionach Chłopskich [Guerrilla Weapons: On Armament in the Peasant Battalions] (Warszawa: People's Publishing Cooperative, 1980), https://www.amazon.com/Partyzancka-broń-uzbrojeniu-Batalionach-Chlopskich/dp/8320532019/ref=sr_1_1?dchild=1&keywords=Bogumił+Karaszewski&qid=1620063878&s=books&sr=1-1.
175 Ryszard Terlecki, Miecz I Tarcza Komunizmu [The Sword and Shield of Communism] (Literary Publishing), accessed May 3, 2021, https://www.amazon.com/tarcza-komunizmu-Polska-wersja-jezy-kowa/dp/B00C47VUZG/ref=sr_1_3?dchild=1&keywords=Ryszard+Terlecki&qid=1620066111&sr=8-3.
176 Adam Leszczynski, "How the NSZ Fought: Attempts to Cooperate with the Germans, Robberies, Attacks on the Home Army.," OKO Press, September 24, 2017, https://oko.press/walczylo-nsz-wspolpraca-niemcami-rabunki-ataki-ak-publikujemy-dokumenty/.
177 Glenn E. Curtis, Poland: A Country Study, Area Handbook Series (Library of Congress Federal Research Division), accessed April 19, 2021, http://countrystudies.us/poland/15.htm.

(ORMO).[178] The Polish army then merged into the Warsaw Pact, while units like the ZOMO squads operated as a paramilitary-riot squad.[179] With the paramilitaries from the previous regime eliminated, Poland consolidated its socialist paramilitaries in their place.

However, the late 1940s was a low-intensity Polish civil war, as an armed struggle between the waning nationalist factions and predominant socialists ensued. From 1945 to 1953, these cursed soldiers of Polish nationalism comprised groups like the National Military Union, Home Army Resistance Movement, and the Polish Underground Army, which all fought against socialist state forces after WW II.[180] The nationalist paramilitaries or so-called reactionary underworld formed to harass socialist strongholds. They continued to use forest people style tactics in the 1950s to murder and sabotage the Citizen's Militia, ORMO, and socialist collaborators within the Polish Workers Party, as they had done during the war.[181] Many of these Polish nationalists were mercilessly hunted down and assassinated or arrested, and sent to gulags during the period. The eradication of the reactionary underworld essentially ended the armed nationalist struggle around 1963.[182] The nationalists switched to civil resistance tactics such as protests and workers strikes from that point onwards. However, the protests and strikes failed due to Citizens Militia or the Polish People's Army interventions

178 Piotr Osęka, "Jak ORMO czuwało [How ORMO Was Watching]," Polityka, February 19, 2011, https://www.polityka.pl/tygodnikpolityka/historia/1513094,1,jak-ormo-czuwalo.read.
179 Andrzej Paczkowski and Malcolm Byrne, From Solidarity to Martial Law: The Polish Crisis of 1980–1981 (Central European University Press, 2007).
180 Doomed Soldiers, "Anti-Communist Underground In Poland 1944-1963," accessed May 3, 2021, http://www.doomedsoldiers.com/introduction.html.
181 PWN Encyclopedia, "Freedom and Independence Association," accessed May 3, 2021, https://encyklopedia.pwn.pl/haslo/;4002133.
182 Doomed Soldiers, "Anti-Communist Underground In Poland 1944-1963."

throughout the Soviet occupation.[183] The paramilitaries of People's Poland maintained little similarity with their pre-socialist counterparts.

With the Soviet collapse, the former buffer states of Central Europe declared independence and instituted national militaries more in line with western standards. In the case of the new Republic of Poland, the military could be seen as legitimate heirs to the previous Polish republic with its actions symbolizing the will of the duly elected politicians and responsible to Warsaw, not Moscow. With the creation of the current Polish state, ZS Strzelec reemerged in 1990 along with other groups under loose democratic supervision.[184] These post-Soviet Polish militias have been virulently anti-communist since independence.

The paramilitary organizations then retrenched a belief they were defenders of Polish sovereignty, as they were again allowed to look back at their origin story of the interwar period.[185] In addition, defense spending waned after Russia and East Europe transitioned to democracy, creating a need for paramilitarism in the minds of would-be members.[186] Concurrently, Poland made political and military reforms to join NATO and the EU during the 1990s. Part of the process was establishing democratic civil control of the military instead of communist dictation to the Polish officer corps.[187] The Polish military went

---

183 PWN Encyclopedia, "Freedom and Independence Association."
184 Webra International, "The Visegrad Group: Polish Paramilitaries - Training to War in Times of Peace," text ((C) 2006-2010, International Visegrad Fund, December 9, 2016), https://www.visegradgroup.eu/polish-paramilitaries.
185 Bartłomiej Kamínski, The Collapse of State Socialism: The Case of Poland (Princeton University Press, 1991), https://www.jstor.org/stable/j.ctt7ztrrc.
186 Jan Śpiewak, "Poland Mobilises Controversial 'Weekend Warriors' for Pandemic Response," Balkan Insight, November 5, 2020, https://balkaninsight.com/2020/11/05/poland-mobilises-controversial-weekend-warriors-for-pandemic-response/.
187 Szemerkényi, Réka. Central European Civil-Military Reforms at Risk : Progress in Establishing Democratic Controls over the Military Has Not Been Sustained . Oxford, [England] ;: Oxford University Press for the International Institute for Strategic Studies, 1996.

on to participate in peacekeeping missions per Warsaw's political objectives.

One important objective was to build ties with the West, notably by operating in support of various NATO or American campaigns.[188] Warsaw sent several contingents supporting the 1991 Gulf War, then NATO peacekeeping missions in Yugoslavia from 1992 to 1995, and the Kosovo campaign in 1999.[189] The subsequent engagements assisted the United States when NATO invoked Article 5 for the first time after the September 11th attacks.[190] The Polish military contingent in Afghanistan started with 100 people but reached 2,600 troops when President Obama initiated his troop surge.[191] These contributions to United States war efforts represented some of the largest in Europe. Secretary of Defense Donald Rumsfeld lauded Polish cooperation when he contrasted their willingness with old Europe, whose center of gravity was quickly shifting East.[192] The 1990s solidified the new democratic control of the Polish national military more in line with western thought. The reorganized political terrain temporarily disrupted pathological aspects of far-left and -right paramilitarism. Bumps and shocks of the 2010s would present new challenges for Poland to respond.

B.   MAJOR EVENTS SINCE 2014

The effect of the European crises of 2014–2015 in Poland differed from Germany regarding Muslim migrants. Poland's migration

---

188 "Missions," Ministry of National Defence, accessed July 7, 2021, https://www.gov.pl/web/national-defence/missions.
189 "Missions."
190 "Missions."
191 "Missions."
192 Defence Secy Comments on Europe, France, Germany, video, 2003, https://www.youtube.com/watch?v=E0GnRJEPXn4.

policy during the situation could not have been more restrictive to middle eastern migrants.[193] Poland's policies contrasted with the country's own experiences with migration from Poland to West Europe or from Ukraine to Poland when many Ukrainians left for Poland.[194] When the middle eastern wave of migration hit, Poland and the other Visegrad countries (Czechia, Hungary, Slovakia) changed sharply toward restrictionism.[195] Specifically, Poland rejected an EU plan to distribute migrants across member states.[196] In 2015, PiS won the majority of *Sejm* (Polish parliament) seats with a mandate to reject immigration to Poland.[197] Further Islamic terror attacks in West Europe further solidified the Polish position.[198] The similarity between Germany's AfD and Poland's PiS was apparent in their restrictionist immigration policies as platform points. The parties differ because Germany had a more sophisticated democracy willing to compromise with other EU member states. As a result, AfD remained a fringe party in Germany while PiS was able to project other aspects of their platform due to capitalization on the migration issue in Poland.

Poland saw Russian annexation as a significant threat to its security, which altered Poland's military preparedness.[199] Evidence for

193 Polska Times, "Fala Uchodźców?"
194 Shaun Walker, "A Whole Generation Has Gone: Ukrainians Seek Better Life in Poland," Guardian, April 18, 2019, http://www.theguardian.com/world/2019/apr/18/whole-generation-has-gone-ukrainian-seek-better-life-poland-elect-president.
195 Polska Times, "Fala Uchodźców?"
196 Bart Bachman, "Diminishing Solidarity: Polish Attitudes toward the European Migration and Refugee Crisis," Migrationpolicy.Org (blog), June 15, 2016, https://www.migrationpolicy.org/article/diminishing-solidarity-polish-attitudes-toward-european-migration-and-refugee-crisis.
197 Guardian, "Rightwing Law and Justice Party Wins Overall Majority in Polish Election," October 27, 2015, http://www.theguardian.com/world/2015/oct/27/poland-law-justice-party-wins-235-seats-can-govern-alone.
198 Bachman, "Diminishing Solidarity."
199 "Poland and Baltics Feel Heat from Crimea," BBC News, March 12, 2014, https://www.bbc.com/news/world-europe-26526053.

this is Poland's 2014 statements advocating for Russia to respect Ukraine's territory and the international system of law.[200] Polish and Lithuanian Presidents went on to demand NATO Article 4 consultations.[201] They reasoned that Poland and the Baltic would be likely next targets for Russian aggression. NATO Secretary-General Anders Rasmussen convened the North Atlantic Council to discuss the issue and reassure those countries.[202] Furthermore, the United States moved several fighters and aerial tankers into Poland to increase combat air patrol capability.[203] To further enhance regional security, in 2015, NATO implemented the Very High Readiness Joint Task Force (VJTF) to place thousands of troops anywhere in Europe within 48 hours.[204] These moves indicated the severity of the situation in the minds of the Polish policymakers.

The Polish paramilitary program since 2015 followed a broader trend in Europe since 2014. The Crimean annexation saw Ukraine deputize its paramilitary forces into the Ukrainian army because Ukraine was unprepared for conflict and desperately needed support.[205] By regimenting its paramilitary volunteers, Poland intended to leverage them against Russia's little green men hybrid war strategy. Poland considered

200 Polish Ministry of Foreign Affairs, "MFA Statement on the Sixth Anniversary of Russia's Annexation of Crimea," Ministry of Foreign Affairs Republic of Poland, March 16, 2020, https://www.gov.pl/web/diplomacy/mfa-statement-on-the-sixth-anniversary-of-russias-annexation-of-crimea.
201 "Lithuanian and Polish Presidents Call For NATO Treaty Article 4 Consultations," Lithuania Tribune, March 7, 2014, https://web.archive.org/web/20140307142447/http://www.lithuaniatribune.com/64476/lithuanian-polish-presidents-call-for-nato-treaty-article-4-consultations-201464476/.
202 NATO, "Statement to the Media by the NATO Secretary General at the Press Conference Held at NATO HQ, Brussels after the Meeting of the NATO-Ukraine Commission," NATO, accessed July 20, 2021,
http://www.nato.int/cps/en/natohq/opinions_107682.htm.
203 BBC News, "Poland and Baltics Feel Heat from Crimea."
204 NATO, "NATO's New Spearhead Force Conducts First Exercise," NATO, accessed July 8, 2021, http://www.nato.int/cps/en/natohq/news_118667.htm.
205 Vasovic and Kiselyova, "Russian Forces Seize Two Ukrainian Bases in Crimea."

the likely target to be along Poland's Northeast frontier as NATO war-gaming suggested Russia will attack the Baltic states along the Suwalki Gap (Polish-Lithuanian border).[206] The addition of paramilitary capacity and the VJTF would maintain state functioning in the critical hours and days following such an attack. Specifically, the paramilitaries are supposed to help with NATO staging and civil response even though Ukraine's Azov Battalion was composed of combatants who secured key locations from Russian separatists in Ukraine.[207] Poland interprets the Crimean involvement as a cautionary tale, which motivated preparations.

C. POLISH RIGHT-WING LANDSCAPE

The story of Polish policy since 2015 was the triumphant tale of Jarosław Kaczyński and his PiS in office. Kaczyński made his start as an anti-communist in People's Poland; however, he viewed democracy as nice-to-have but not essential. Like Piłsudski before him, he considered himself a Polish patriot, eyeing numerous European threats to Polish independence, which democracy may weaken in times of crisis.[208] Furthermore, from 2006 to 2007, Kaczyński was Prime Minister and remained Poland's leading political figure since his time in office.[209] In 2010, Jarosław's twin brother, Lech Kaczyński, died as President

---

206 NATO, "Readiness Action Plan."

207 "Ukraine's Most-Feared Volunteers," BBC News, February 27, 2015, https://www.bbc.com/news/av/world-europe-31657354.

208 Jan Śpiewak, "Jarosław Kaczyński, Czyli Naczelnik Naszych Czasów - Ranking Najbardziej Wpływowych [Jarosław Kaczyński, The Chief of Our Time - Ranking of The Most Influential]," Wprost, October 27, 2019, https://www.wprost.pl/tygodnik/10264563/jaroslaw-kaczynski-czyli-naczelnik-naszych-czasow-ranking-najbardziej-wplywowych.html.

209 "Jarosław Kaczyński zapowiedziany jako Naczelnik Państwa [Jarosław Kaczyński Announced as the Head of State}," Onet Wiadomości, 45:56 100AD, https://wiadomosci.onet.pl/kraj/jaroslaw-kaczynski-zapowiedziany-jako-naczelnik-panstwa/jvest9.

with several senior military officers in an airplane accident near Smolensk, Russia.[210] Lech's intended visit was to commemorate the Katyn massacre perpetrated by Russians in WW II. The aircraft's failure over the Russian city of Smolensk fanned conspiracy theories amongst Poland's far-right who assumed Russian foul play.[211] Jarosław Kaczyński stated the crash was a political assassination.[212] The contemporary Polish right distrusts Russia because of its historical dominance, but PiS has creates a cult around Lech's mysterious death as a justification for anti-Russian rhetoric.

Like in the other Visegrád countries, there have been some strong right-ward shifts.[213] PiS formed a governing coalition consisting of the right-wing parties, United Poland, and Agreement. United Poland began with former PiS members who questioned PiS leadership after failing to win certain elections.[214] United Poland emphasized its conservative, anti-gay, pro-family stance.[215] The Agreement Party, another PiS breakaway, emphasized a non-interventionist economic

---

210 Monika Sieradzka, "Smolensk: The Tragedy That Defined Polish Politics," Deutsche Welle, October 4, 2018, https://www.dw.com/en/smolensk-the-tragedy-that-defined-polish-politics/a-43328611.
211 Sieradzka.
212 Sieradzka.
213 Jonathan Katz and Torrey Taussig, "An Inconvenient Truth: Addressing Democratic Backsliding within NATO," Brookings (blog), July 10, 2018, https://www.brookings.edu/blog/order-from-chaos/2018/07/10/an-inconvenient-truth-addressing-democratic-backsliding-within-nato/.
214 Radio Poland, "New Polish Conservative Party Launched," Polskie Radio dla Zagranicy, March 26, 2012, http://archiwum.thenews.pl/1/9/Artykul/94458,New-Polish-conservative-party-launched.
215 Radio Poland.

stance while taking a softer tone on cultural questions.[216] Together, PiS and associates formed the ruling political milieu of Poland.

When PiS came to power, many lingering communists were subject to firings. In 2017, PiS began shaking up the military establishment by replacing many Admirals at the Polish Naval Academy due to their communist pasts.[217] The National Defense Academy and the Dęblin Air Force Officer School were similarly affected. The instance at the National Defense Academy saw the Commanding Officer and then 103 other employees dismissed.[218] PiS doubted the Commanding Officer's ideological commitment to their nationalist objectives since he and many others matured under the communist system.[219] However, its noted that Communist Party membership was often a requisite for high office during socialist rule.[220] The political death, extraction, and replacement with card-holding PiS members would be a recurrent feature of PiS-ruled Poland.

PiS had gone on to make other controversial political appointments, which legitimized fringe paramilitary figures. In one instance, Thomasz Grenuich, former leader of the National Radical Camp (*Obóz Narodowo-Radykalny*, ONR), became the leader of Wrocław's Institute

---

216 Tomasz Gzell, "Gowin: '4 listopada podczas kongresu Polski Razem zostanie zaprezentowana nowa formacja polityczna' [Gowin: 'On November 4, during the Polish Congress Together, a New Political Formation Will Be Presented']," wPolityce.pl, October 13, 2017, https://wpolityce.pl/polityka/362191-gowin-4-listopada-podczas-kongresu-polski-razem-zostanie-zaprezentowana-nowa-formacja-polityczna?strona=1.
217 Edyta Zemla, "Admirałowie Usunięci z Akademii Marynarki Wojennej [Admirals Removed from the Naval Academy]," Onet Wiadomości, 39:24 100AD, https://wiadomosci.onet.pl/tylko-w-onecie/admiralowie-usunieci-z-akademii-marynarki-wojennej/q3b710m.
218 Zemla.
219 Zemla.
220 Theodore P. Gerber, "Membership Benefits or Selection Effects? Why Former Communist Party Members Do Better in Post-Soviet Russia," Social Science Research 29, no. 1 (March 1, 2000): 25–50, https://doi.org/10.1006/ssre.1999.0651.

for National Remembrance.[221] Grenuich previously attended neo-Nazi marches, gave Hitler salutes that ended up on social media, and even published a book titled, The Way of The Nationalist, which praises WW II Nazi collaborators.[222] In another case, Adam Adnruszkiewicz, former president of the nationalist All-Polish Youth, was appointed as Poland's deputy minister of digital affairs.[223] The American Jewish Committee protested his appointment to Poland's top spot for online hate speech due to his far-right activity.[224] Finally, PiS appointed Bartłomiej Zborski of National Revival of Poland (*Narodowe Odrodzenie Polski*, NOP) to be a Ministry of National Defense author and editor— despite his high-profile work as a Holocaust denial specialist.[225] These political appointments represent the linkage between Poland's far-right paramilitaries and the PiS government to man government posts with far-right paramilitarists at the expense of more experienced but less ideologically aligned individuals.

PiS had gone further to militarize the civilian population in some radical ways for an EU member state. A 2017 bill introduced by Republican party MP Anna Maria Siarkowska intended to start the

221 Ben Cohen, "Fury over Polish Government's Appointment of Former Far Right '100% Aryan' Activist to Leading State Post," Algemeiner.com, February 18, 2021, https://www.algemeiner.com/2021/02/18/fury-over-polish-governments-appoint-ment-of-former-far-right-100-aryan-activist-to-leading-state-post/.
222 Cohen.
223 "Ex-Hate Group Leader Tasked with Fighting Hate Speech in Poland, Jewish Group Says," Haaretz.com, accessed July 9, 2021, https://www.haaretz.com/world-news/europe/ex-hate-group-leader-tasked-with-fighting-hate-speech-in-poland-jew-ish-group-says-1.6823492.
224 "Ex-Hate Group Leader Tasked with Fighting Hate Speech in Poland, Jewish Group Says."
225 Rafal Pankowski, "Right-Wing Extremism in Poland," International Policy Analysis (Bonn: Friedrich Ebert Foundation, October 2012), https://library.fes.de/pdf-files/id-moe/09409-20121029.pdf.

school arms program.[226] The bill planned to teach marksmanship and gun safety in primary school classrooms and enable the Pro-defense Organizations to use machine guns. The Pro-defense Organization was a term of art created by Polish authority to reconceptualize a paramilitary organization. The bill also intended to increase firearm ownership in Poland from 440,000 firearms to 1,000,000 firearms.[227] The bill attracted advocacy from international shooting organizations like Firearms United Network's President Tomasz Stępień.[228] Stępień was a significant figure in the European gun liberalization debate.[229] These pro-gun initiatives represent the Polish military attitude of late.

Poland was also an epicenter for private security contractor training, commonly known as Private Military Companies (PMCs). One example of this is the Wrocław-based European Security Academy.[230] The European Security Academy trained security detail members, but its services extended to paramilitary training with a Polish ideological commitment. A Soufan Center report showed the severity of the phenomenon in other ways. No fewer than 25 Polish paramilitarists fought in Ukraine between 2014 and 2019.[231] An International Centre for Counter-Terrorism report estimates that between 20 and 40 Poles were active in Iraq and Syrian conflict zones as of 2016.[232] These

---

226 Daniel Flis and Anna Gielewska, "Pro-Defense Organizations Want Real Guns," Vsquare.Org, January 21, 2019, https://vsquare.org/pro-defense-organizations-want-real-guns/.

227 Flis and Gielewska.

228 Flis and Gielewska.

229 Firearms United Network, "Tomasz W. Stępień, President of Firearms United, Delivered A Fiery Closing Remark," accessed June 4, 2021, https://firearms-united.com/stepien/.

230 European Security Academy, "ESA - Home Page," European Security Academy, April 2021, https://www.euseca.com/.

231 Blazakis et al., "White Supremacy Extremism."

232 Bibi van Ginkel et al., "The Foreign Fighters Phenomenon in the European Union. Profiles, Threats & Policies," ed. Eva Entenmann, Terrorism and Counter-Terrorism Studies, April 1, 2016, https://doi.org/10.19165/2016.1.02.

measures represented the lack of control PiS had in its defense needs amid Russian threats to Poland's periphery. Polish militarism at the societal level is pervasive but, it also confirms the far-right suspicion that Russia could attack again. PiS and the paramilitaries capitalize on the fear to further an anti-liberal platform in Polish politics. However, the far-right platform does not bode well for democratic consolidation in transition to the 21st century amid a grey-zone struggle.

D. POLISH PARAMILITARIES

The Polish paramilitary stood out for how mainstream it was and how paramilitarism translates into Polish white ethnonationalism. Instead of a fringe phenomenon as it was in Germany or Sweden, its Presidential nods and political appointments legitimized them. One important tool for the Polish paramilitaries was their demonstration rallies that suggested their ideas were patriotic and normal. A 2017 Independence Day march had 60,000 attendees. The state television service TVP broadcasted the PiS Interior Minister's comment that the crowd's patriotism was a beautiful sight.[233] A 2018 march through Warsaw witnessed a larger far-right demonstration with 100,000 people having attended.[234] The attendees chanted slogans like "Poland can't be red or rainbow, Poland must be nationalist!"[235] The marchers donned patriotic shirts with Polish Hussar cavalry while styling Poles and especially the far-right as Defenders of Europe.[236]

---

233 Paul Hockenos, "Poland and the Uncontrollable Fury of Europe's Far-Right," The Atlantic, November 15, 2017, https://www.theatlantic.com/international/archive/2017/11/europe-far-right-populist-nazi-poland/524559/.

234 Konrad Szczygiel, "T-Shirts Made in Poland. Not in the European Union," Vsquare.Org, January 22, 2019, https://vsquare.org/t-shirts-made-in-poland-not-in-the-eu/.

235 Szczygiel.

236 Szczygiel.

The march's primary clothing purveyor was the Red Is Bad brand and is central to the Polish far right. Red Is Bad extols the fact its clothing was Polish-made for the Polish.[237] The far-right brand elevated its popular political support among the right when President Duda wore one of their T-shirts to visit China.[238] In 2018, Polish President Morawiecki toured a Red Is Bad store on the anniversary of the 74th Warsaw Uprising.[239] The company's founders are right-wing, Eurosceptic, and highly critical of Polish foreign policy.[240] The paramilitary groups sponsor and promote these marches.[241] The clothing brand, paramilitaries, and elements of the Polish executive branch are a cohesive political force.

The fertile political landscape allowed the pro-Polish paramilitary groups like the National Rebirth of Poland (NOP). The NOP's website's stated goals were for action toward the Third Position associated with spiritualism along Catholic lines and rejection of liberal rights like abortion, homosexuality, and opposition to deleterious institutions in Freemasonry, laissez-faire capitalism, Marxism, and Zionism. NOP advocated for racial separatism from non-Poles, and a robust Polish state avoidant of supranational entanglements.[242] NOP operated as a political party to publish material but held no seats in the Sejm. While Article 13 of the Polish Constitution put restrictions on extrem-

---

237 Szczygiel.
238 Szczygiel.
239 Pudelek, Dumny Morawiecki Przechadza Się Po Sklepie z Odzieżą Patriotyczną [The Proud Morawiecki Strolls Through The Patriotic Clothing Store] (Poland, 2018), https://www.youtube.com/watch?v=8yRnmH4UVgM.
240 Szczygiel, "T-Shirts Made in Poland. Not in the European Union."
241 Michał Broniatowski and David M. Herszenhorn, "White Nationalists Call For Ethnic Purity at Polish Demonstration," Politico, November 12, 2017, https://www.politico.eu/article/white-nationalists-call-for-ethnic-purity-at-polish-independence-day-march/.
242 "ONR Deklaracja Ideowa [ONR Ideological Declaration]," Obóz Narodowo-Radykalny, accessed April 19, 2021, https://www.onr.com.pl/deklaracja-ideowa/.

ist activity, only the NOP chapter based in the city of Brzeg experienced a ban.[243] NOP is quite popular but also dangerous, so PiS must pulse-check NOP for threats from time to time.

In 2015, one NOP member, Brunon Kwiecień, was convicted of politically-motivated terrorism. His intended plan was to use an explosives-laden personnel carrier to destroy the Sejm building while the President and Prime Minister attended.[244] The NOP website characterizes Kwiecień's trial as a miscarriage of justice and a plot from Poland's Internal Security Agency to discredit the individual to expand the state's power.[245] PiS has been careful to keep NOP under its influence, but these lone-wolf attackers present further challenges for the party. PiS maintains a careful balance between realpolitik state interest and far-right credibility.

Phalanx (*Falanga*) fit a different model because it was a pan-Slavic, pro-Russian paramilitary group working against the Polish state. Phalanx's founding dates back before WW II when it was an anti-Semitic, nationalist group under the National Radical Camp (ONR) umbrella.[246] Its website denoted similar platitudes as ONR and NOP but

243 Pankowski, "Right-Wing Extremism in Poland."
244 Agencja Gazeta, "Wyrok W Sprawie Przygotowania Zamachu NA Sejm: Brunon Kwiecień Skazany NA 13 Lat WIęZienia [The Verdict on the Preparation of the Attack on the Seym: Brunon Kwiecień Sentenced to 13 Years in Prison]," Dziennik.pl, December 21, 2015, https://wiadomosci.dziennik.pl/wydarzenia/artykuly/508750,jest-wyrok-w-sprawie-brunona-kwietnia-mezczyzna-skazany-na-13-lat-wiezienia.html.
245 National Rebirth of Poland, "Brunon April - Present!," Narodowe Odrodzenie Polski (NOP) – Nacjonalistyczna Opozycja (blog), accessed June 5, 2021, https://www.nop.org.pl/2020/08/06/brunon-kwiecien-obecny/.
246 Jerzy Holzer, "The Political Right in Poland, 1918-39," Journal of Contemporary History 12, no. 3 (1977): 395–412.

with more pronounced disapproval of the Sejm and democracy in general.[247] Unlike the previous two groups, which are critical but supportive of Poland, Falanga was not loyal to Polish democratic institutions. Phalanx proclaims that NATO was an occupation force in Poland and the United States was the true evil empire.[248] One article describes how in 2018, Phalanx found a loophole to participate in NATO's Operation Anakonda to the dismay of the United States Army.[249] Phalanx's participation was not accepted because the United States Army would not work with paramilitaries, instead opting to only cooperate with state-controlled conventional forces. The article concludes that Poland's MoD has done a poor job vetting paramilitary groups citing Phalanx's receipt of the all-important Passport to participate in the NATO exercise.

In 2019, Phalanx's leader and founder Bartosz Bekeier spoke at the Russian Duma.[250] He advocated for Poland to leave both the EU and NATO to ally with Russia. Bekier wants Ukraine to cede the Donetsk Republic to Russian influence and for Poland to annex the Ukrainian city of L'viv. Bekier has been a critical node in Polish paramilitarists traveling to Syria and Ukraine's Donetsk combat zone. Phalanx conducted armed patrols along the Polish-Ukrainian border to engage Ukrainian targets.[251] Phalanx is one of Poland's most urgent paramilitary threats, and one should expect them to cooperate with Russian hybrid warfare strategies should a move against Poland or the Baltics occur.

---

247 "Dziesięć haseł polskiego falangizmu [10 Slogans of Polish Phalanxism]," Xportal.pl (blog), March 28, 2017, https://xportal.pl/?p=28865.
248 Falanga.
249 Konrad Szczygiel, "Millions for Uniforms," Vsquare.Org, March 4, 2019, https://vsquare.org/millions-for-uniforms/.
250 Przemyslaw Witkowski, "In Moscow, the Leader of the Fascist Falanga Calls for Lviv to Join Poland," OKO Press, August 30, 2019, https://oko.press/lider-faszyzujacej-falangi-domaga-sie-w-moskwie-przylaczenia-do-polski-lwowa/#.
251 Witkowski.

E.   STATE-PARAMILITARY CONNECTION

In response to the Crimean annexation, the Polish government seeks to incorporate some of its Pro-defense Organizations, like how Ukraine has during its annexation. To this end, Polish officials establish the Territorial Defense Force (*Wojska Obrony Terytorialnej*, WOT) with the Polish MoD as their supervisory bureau.[252] One WOT Private First Class describes his motivations: "I wanted to learn in peacetime what the Ukrainians had learned in war."[253] The Polish government website describes WOT as an amalgam of professional and part-time soldiers protecting their local communities in supporting Poland's defense needs and NATO's Article 3 requirement to build defense capability.[254] WOT's establishment is a profound step for a NATO member state to make and is unique to Poland in that regard.

The Polish military magazine *Polska Zbrojna* elaborates what WOT endeavors to accomplish as a new paramilitary force. In 2017, starts with a goal of 50,000 soldiers.[255] Only 10 percent of these soldiers are professional members of the Polish army; the rest are volunteer reservists but provides 30 days of professional training per year. According to the Polish government website, the minimum requirements to join WOT are Polish citizenship, no criminal background, and a primary education.[256] By joining WOT, a recruit undergoes 30 training days a year as individual training the first year. Graduates specialize in

---

252 Ministry of National Defense, "Territorial Defense Forces," Ministry of National Defense, accessed June 3, 2021, https://www.gov.pl/web/national-defence/territorial-defence-forces.
253 Śpiewak, "Poland Mobilises Controversial 'Weekend Warriors' for Pandemic Response."
254 Ministry of National Defense, "Territorial Defense Forces."
255 Paulina Glińska and Magdalena Kowalska-Sendek, "WOT - Mission, Structure, Training," May 21, 2017, http://www.polska-zbrojna.pl/home/articleshow/22674?t=WOT-misja-struktura-szkolenie#.
256 Ministry of National Defense, "Territorial Defence Forces," Ministry of National Defense, accessed June 3, 2021, https://www.gov.pl/web/national-defence/territorial-defence-forces.

a specific infantry weapon capability like crew-served weapons or mortars in the second year, and finally, operate as integrated infantry in the third year.[257] The WOT programs show Polish authorities tap into youth patriotism to supplement the Polish security situation.

An article by Matej Kandrík from the German Marshall Fund maps the Polish paramilitary implementation. He classifies Polish paramilitaries as decentralized non-state networks in the vein of ZS Strzelec.[258] Paramilitary units can augment the Polish army with a co-operation agreement known as the Passport.[259] The Passport allows paramilitary members to use military shooting ranges and training facilities.[260] The paramilitaries will drill light infantry tactics, urban warfare, and medical triage/evacuation. As part of civil services extension, the paramilitaries clean national monuments, offer civic parade services, offer food drive support, and donate blood.[261] Passport members participation in two NATO exercises between 2017 and 2018 is a first.[262] Kandrík describes the inception of WOT as a milestone for Polish paramilitarists due to the state's legitimization of the paramilitary culture in Polish society.[263] The following image is a photograph from 2017 showing the WOT's new soldiers as part of the planned paramilitary defense.

---

257 Glińska and Kowalska-Sendek, "WOT - Mission, Structure, Training."
258 Matej Kandrík, "The Challenge of Paramilitarism in Central and Eastern Europe" (German Marshall Fund of the United States, 2020), http://www.jstor.org/stable/resrep26757.
259 Kandrík.
260 Kandrík.
261 Kandrík.
262 Kandrík.
263 Kandrík.

Figure 3.   Territorial Defense Force formed for inspection.[264]

F.   POLISH RESPONSE TO PARAMILITARISM

The Federation of Pro-Defense Organizations is the organizing body of government concerning paramilitary affairs. Since 2014, the Federation of Pro-Defense and WOT is a product of PiS party thinking on defense.[265] Because the PiS majority government institutes the WOT, PiS's close association with far-right paramilitary groups prompts controversy. The center-right Civic Platform party associates with former Polish Prime Minister Donald Tusk calls for their standing down due to their extremist connections.[266] Civic Platform worries the

264 Silar, WOT-Soldaten, Karpatenvorland-Brigade [WOT Soldiers, Subcarpathian Brigade], September 24, 2017, September 24, 2017, Own work, https://com-mons.wikimedia.org/wiki/File:02017_0074_Karpatenvorland-WOT-Brigade.jpg.
265 Śpiewak, "Poland Mobilises Controversial 'Weekend Warriors' for Pandemic Response."
266 Śpiewak.

paramilitaries would take on a lawless, vigilante character in Poland.[267] Yet, Polska Zbrojna states the paramilitary program will strengthen Poland's defense by uniting the many groups.[268] The article says that the Pro-Defense Organization aims to instill patriotism and galvanize defense attitudes toward support for the defense efforts.[269] By other accounts, the Federation of Pro-defense organizations has done a commendable job establishing the system.

However, Poland's paramilitary system is not without faults. From 2014 to 2015, Major General Pacek acts as the defense organization's founding leader.[270] He says the Federation of Pro-Defense should be like Switzerland in its patriotic instruction and preparation in military matters.[271] However, a 2018 investigation shows the government is not getting much return on investment.[272] By 2018, only 184 people of the 6,216 WOT volunteers come from Pro-defense Organizations, and the rest are civilians with no paramilitary associations. Another problem is that paramilitary orders like Phalanx are not only anti-Semitic but are distinctly pro-Russia and anti-NATO, though they still occupy a spot on the payroll. One article states that PiS is trying to legitimize the WOT and the Federation of Pro-Defense by activating both for the Covid-19 response.[273] Using the paramilitaries in these civically beneficial ways might be a savvy public relations move, but it also reveals

---

267 Śpiewak.
268 Małgorzata Schwarzgruber, "The Federation of Pro-Defense Organizations Was Established," March 21, 2015, http://www.polska-zbrojna.pl/home/articleshow/15466?t=Powstala-Federacja-Organizacji-Proobronnych#.
269 Schwarzgruber.
270 Schwarzgruber.
271 Schwarzgruber.
272 Szczygiel, "Millions for Uniforms."
273 Śpiewak, "Poland Mobilises Controversial 'Weekend Warriors' for Pandemic Response."

government failure in budgeting for medical, police, and firefighter services.[274] These examples show how well-intended the paramilitaries might be, and they are far from providing a rubric for the rest of Europe to copy.

Kandrík commends the Polish model for its accessibility for would-be recruits into civic participation under legitimate state supervision.[275] The civic-patriotic groups provide a hedging strategy against the extremist variety of paramilitarism, especially for teenage members. Kandrík recommends a holistic assessment of paramilitary groups where activity is checked against national laws.[276] Extremism, hate crimes, illegal firearm possession, and co-opting military uniforms could be the basis of assessment for state authorities looking to eliminate bad actors. Groups in violation could have funding cut or their Passport revoked to encourage changes.[277] Further intelligence, police, and military counterintelligence should provide civilian leadership with analysis of these organizations' strengths, weaknesses, opportunities, and threats. Kandrík states that another problem is that Poland lacks legal definition for paramilitaries.[278] Legal efforts to enforce and prosecute where needed are frustrated because the current arrangement has an informal quality. These elements of the system serve as focal points for the improvement of the paramilitary system.

Kandrík also points out that the extremist paramilitary variant is flourishing, and the Russian hybrid war could complicate their arrangement during times of crisis, possibly acting as a fifth column.[279] Poland has done much with its budget and population, but it must continue to do more to increase its security. Polish democracy stands in

---

274 Śpiewak.
275 Kandrík, "The Challenge of Paramilitarism in Central and Eastern Europe."
276 Kandrík.
277 Kandrík.
278 Kandrík.
279 Kandrík.

opposition to the Russian model of governance, so Poland is a target. The paramilitary connection to the Law and Justice makes a change in governing coalition a challenge to Polish defense in the current arrangement. If a center-left government comes to power, the paramilitary system would be in danger, so it follows that the paramilitary units might become a security concern themselves.

G.   DISCUSSION

Poland has an understandably strong connection to paramilitarism, but a changing world awaits them. Poland retains the vestige as a guarantee in the current context of NATO and the EU. The problem, therefore, is how the relationship between state and militia is conducive to societal growth and strong democratic institutions. Poland must continue to balance its military, people, and government effectively. The government maintains popular support and security by cultivating the citizen militia. The military gains an auxiliary force and recruits to help the government institutions retain coherence during security challenges. But are these developments sustainable and good for democracy? Is it a good model for the rest of the EU after Poland perfects it? Returning to Janowitzian concepts, Poland is a militarized society. Poland is a NATO member too, so its high-ranking officers interfacing with NATO for Polish defense are selected for pragmaticism. But the shift in armament in Poland could suggest a change in thinking, possibly toward the absolutist mindset.

Except for the pro-Russian Phalanx paramilitary, Poland sees its paramilitaries as central to its opposition to Russian revisionism, so it has struck a unique bargain with its people. To prepare for the ever-present Russian threat, Poles rely on the far-right more than most. The Polish Republic is also more illiberal in Europe, so its right-wing government is much more comfortable with its far-right fringe than would be possible in Germany. Poland's commitment to nationalism, conservatism, and militarization might also be a warning sign for fascism elsewhere. But Poland can improve by taking a state-led approach to its paramilitarism. Poland must take its Pro-defense Organization under more direct supervision to be helpful in military tasking while eliminating its more pathological elements. Furthermore, the Polish government must address the crucial aspect of the Russian hybrid war: European disintegration. The Russian strategy for reordering Central Europe depends on EU-infighting to open the societal gaps for Russia to fill the vacuum of stability. The EU can reconcile with the Polish flare for independence and conservatism. However, the burden of responsibility lies on the Polish authorities to promote values and institutions vital to Polish defense within the European framework. Therefore, more work to promote European integration for the sake of security should top Poland's concerns.

IV. SWEDEN

Sweden has a reputation for stability; however, its paramilitary scene is quickly becoming one of Europe's most influential and dangerous blood-and-soil advocates. The 2014–2015 European crisis enables Sweden's paramilitaries to leverage Russian action in Crimea and changed societal demographics into parliamentary success, which arguably undermines Sweden's security. The populist-right Sweden Democrats (SD) are analogous to AfD in Germany and PiS in Poland, and it is the paramilitary scene's champion looking to exclude immigrants and dissociate from mainland European policies. SD's center of gravity is Sweden's mainstream parties' inability to offer nuanced solutions to Sweden's difficult problems lately. For example, 14 percent of the Swedish population is currently foreign-born, and the country is now experiencing new levels and types of crime.[280] SD wants to reverse those trends, and many Swedes are feeling ambivalent or even buyer's remorse towards the slow integrating migrants. In addition, SD is refocusing the political debate onto defense spending so Sweden can survive as an independent non-NATO country on the Baltic Sea. Other indicators of change appear in 2020 when SD forces out the seven-year incumbent Prime Minister, holds one-third of *Riksdag* (Parliament) seats, and will probably form the governing coalition after the 2022 elections.

Yet, SD is only one piece of the Swedish far-right that is clearly on the rise. Other extremist paramilitary groups are gaining popularity, including the neo-Nazi aligned Nordic Resistance Movement, Nordic Strength, National Future, and the Soldiers of Odin. Surging Swedish paramilitarism means a counter-revolutionary renaissance is underway

---

280 OECD, "Indicators of Integration 2012 - Sweden," accessed August 3, 2021, https://www.oecd.org/migration/integration-indicators-2012/keyindicatorsby-country/name,218347,en.htm.

to the detriment of the integrationist hopes on which European prosperity and security rely.

A.   PARAMILITARY HISTORY

Sweden's history with paramilitarism started as a local and relatively minor phenomenon through the end of World War II. What paramilitarism it did have at the beginning of the 20th century traced to the post-WW I upheaval in the nearby states of Finland and Russia. A paramilitary unit known as the Swedish Brigade of approximately 700 men participated in the Finnish Civil War at the Battle of Tempere, fighting against the Finnish communist forces, which the fledgling Soviet Union supported.[281] Another group, *Munckska kåren* (Munck Corps), which probably numbered several thousand members, was formed in 1927 under the leadership of Army Lieutenant General Bror Munck to prepare a Swedish nationalist insurgency force against socialist revolutionaries coming from Russia.[282] Munckska kåren operated in a gray area where private acknowledgement existed amongst some officials. However, the group was publicly condemned when it was exposed for its stockpiled weapons to use against socialist agitators. The Prime Minister publicly denied any awareness of the group or its machinations. Between 1931 and 1932, the group's leaders were guilty of various crimes, which diminished the groups' membership until it could no longer function.[283] The Munck Corps had almost too much

---

281 Reino Arimo, Saksalaisten sotilaallinen toiminta Suomessa 1918 [German Military Action in Finland 1918] (Rovaniemi: Northern Finnish Historical Soceity, 1991), https://www.amazon.com/Saksalaisten-sotilaallinen-toiminta-historica-septentrionalia/dp/9519617442.

282 Swedish Defense Research Agency (FOI), "Difficult Transition to Democratic Defense," August 25, 2010, https://web.archive.org/web/20100825141814/http://www.foi.se/FOI/templates/Page____560.aspx.

283 Kent Zetterberg, "Brother OC Munck," in Swedish Biographical Dictionary (SBL), accessed February 19, 2021, https://sok.riksarkivet.se/sbl/Presentation.aspx?id=9542.

legitimacy due to its national hero at its top position and its reasoned concern of socialist revolution to pose a significant threat to the Swedish government. That would change as other groups taking their place would pose a more significant threat.

Swedish Nazi parties began forming in the 1930s—for example, the National Socialist Bloc, the Swedish Socialist Coalition, and the Swedish National Socialist Party.[284] These parties resembled the German Nazi party in rhetoric, the donning of paramilitary SA-style uniforms, adapting Swastikas to Swedish flags, and parading in demonstration marches. All these political organizations failed to enter the Swedish Riksdag except for the Nazi-aligned Swedish National Federation, which held three seats from 1934 to 1936.[285] The 1930s Nazi period would inflect the future of Sweden's paramilitaries for generations to come.

Before the German invasion of Norway and Denmark, a deep concern of invasion set in Sweden despite its neutrality. In 1940, the Swedish government instituted its current territorial defense force named the Home Guard (*Hemvärnet*) after the German invasion of Poland.[286] The Home Guard was established from existing shooting associations for additional protection. Sweden was able to remain neutral and uninvaded during WW II, more due to geopolitical concerns of Germany than Sweden's military might. However, the militia remained an integral part of Swedish defense because it could be readily tasked and was inexpensive.

---

284 Heléne Lööw, Nazismen I Sverige 1924 1979: Pionjarerna, Partierna, Propagandan [Nazism in Sweden 1924 1979: The Pioneers, The Parties, Propaganda] (Stockholm: Ordfront, 2004).
285 Lööw.
286 Swedish Armed Forces, "The Home Guard's 80th Anniversary," Försvarsmakten, accessed February 19, 2021, https://www.forsvarsmakten.se/en/news/2020/05/the-home-guards-80th-anniversary/.

Nazi Swedes inspired the post-WW II era well into the late 20th century because the ideology challenged mutual enemies in Leftists and Slavs while championing the northern European people's cause for exclusivity. Scandinavian paramilitaries coopted both ideological quirks and have remained staples of Swedish nationalism since. In the early days of the Cold War, far-right elements were elevated in international importance by clandestine services. These paramilitaries benefitted the state due to their anti-Communist, anti-Soviet covert strategy of preparing stay-behind networks for Sweden's part in Operation Gladio.[287] Sweden's participation in the operation allowed the paramilitaries to store weapons in forests to be used by the Swedish insurgency in the case of Soviet invasion.[288] The post-war environment that the Swedish far-right inherited had discredited their ideology to most of society except for the opposition to communism. Anti-communism allowed a retooled far-right scene to continue legitimate political operations while retaining their vestiges to Nazism.

In 1951, Sweden's political landscape saw the far-right institute their political ideas in the Malmö movement, also known as the European Social Movement, to further the cause of pan-European national socialism. The Malmö movement envisioned building Europe-wide political cooperation toward the tenets of national socialism in the post-war environment while de-emphasizing anti-Semitism.[289] The Malmö movement was closely tied to the charismatic Swedish far-right leader Per Engdahl and his New Swedish Movement. As a subset of the wider European Social Movement, the New Swedish Movement sought to glorify Swedish heritage and distinct culture. The Swedish movement also inspired the 1951 German Social Movement toward

---

287 NATO's Secret Armies.
288 Parallel History Project on Cooperative Security, "Chronology."
289 Geoff Harris, The Dark Side of Europe: The Extreme Right Today, First Edition (Edinburgh: Edinburgh University Press, 1990).

similar goals. These movements represented the first far-right political parties since the 1930s Swedish Nazi parties, so their reimagined national socialism was critical to the far right's political continuity during the Cold War.

In 1953, paramilitarism in the style of SA reemerged with Otto Hallberg.[290] Hallberg was a Swedish volunteer of Finland's anti-Soviet Continuation war who most likely did not know of Operation Gladio's existence or did not think it was adequate, so he began his redundant network. Hallberg attracted far-right Swedes looking to build a stay-behind network outside government control. They took inspiration from Operation *Werwolf*, Nazi Germany's plan to resist allied forces with guerilla forces, which was itself inspired by the Soviet Partisans fighting the Nazis. However, Hallberg's arrest and further investigation of the network caused its collapse.

In 1956, the far-right Nordic National Party attempted to re-create an SA-like paramilitary called the National Action Group (*Riksaktiongruppen*, RAG). The RAG was more of a criminal gang than a purely ideologically motivated paramilitary force.[291] An example of its tactics was an attack on a 1974 Mel Brooks film screening with a smoke bomb.[292] They committed a series of arsons between 1985 and 1986.[293] The remainder of the Cold War through the late 1980s and early 1990s saw the gradual evolution of the paramilitary groups of the present.[294] The scene grew from small clannish groups into associations net-worked with the Anglophone scene, including, for example, the U.S.

---

290 Parallel History Project on Cooperative Security, "Chronology."
291 Daniel Poohl, "Nordiska rikspartiet (NRP) [Nordic National Party (NRP)]," Expo.se, March 7, 2019, https://expo.se/fakta/wiki/nordiska-rikspartiet-nrp.
292 Poohl.
293 Poohl.
294 Anna-Lena Lodenius, Extremhögern [The Far Right] (Stockholm: University Press, 1991).

White Aryan Resistance (WAR) in 1991.[295] The internationalization of the Swedish far-right would be another inflection point for the groups that would further develop the ability harness international engagement in the future.

The Soviet Union's existence likely had the most significant influence on the far-right character from the end of WW II into the 1990s. In the post-war 1950s, East-West tensions were such that the far-right's distrust of the Left was to prepare for war and advance anti-Soviet rhetoric. The demise of the Soviet Union allowed the far-right to spread in a more relaxed environment with fewer state entanglements because many governments, Sweden included, hoped that liberal, democratic systems were ascending in former adversarial countries. But nationalists in the formerly communist countries, along with the far-right in the democratic countries, now had a common purpose to oppose liberal democratic excesses like immigration, cosmopolitanism, and other radical changes to their formerly insular societies.

B. MAJOR EVENTS SINCE 2014

The European migration crisis made much of the current successes of the Swedish far-right possible. SD, PiS, and AfD were once right-wing pariah parties associated with neo-Nazi ideas until their articulation of popular anti-immigrant sentiment met governing coalitions that refused an anti-immigrant policy. Danielle Tomson describes the effect that Sweden's liberal immigration program had on the rise of its populist right party, SD.[296] Specifically, in 2015, immigrants from

---

295 "Nordic Resistance Movement," Counter Extremism Project, accessed July 26, 2021, https://www.counterextremism.com/supremacy/nordic-resistance-movement.

296 Danielle Lee Tomson, "The Rise of Sweden Democrats: Islam, Populism and the End of Swedish Exceptionalism," Brookings (blog), March 25, 2020, https://www.brookings.edu/research/the-rise-of-sweden-democrats-and-the-end-of-swedish-exceptionalism/.

Syria, Iraq, and Afghanistan surged the asylum application system to an equivalent of 1.6 percent of Sweden's 10 million population.[297] This 1.6 percent corresponded to an increase from 30,000 asylum seekers per year to 160,000 over three months in the summer of 2015.[298] Sweden was a popular destination because generous social welfare programs offered assistance for those seeking better lives. The Swedes prided themselves on their ability to help the dispossessed as part of their Swedish exceptionalism, but this enthusiasm was quickly politically exhausted.[299] In November 2015, the formerly open country changed its immigrant quotas to the EU minimum—and reclassified immigrants' visas from permanent to temporary ones.[300] The immigration-focused voter had choices between the anti-immigrant SD or the pro-immigration status quo of the incumbent centrist parties.[301] The choice awarded electoral gains to SD and their anti-immigrant policies with each subsequent election since 2015.[302] As of July 2021, they held a third of parliamentary seats in the Riksdag.[303] The parallels between Germany's AfD and SD became apparent, though SD did much better winning electoral seats than AfD.

The Crimean invasion caused Sweden to rethink its defense capability around this same time frame. When the initial stages of the Crimean incident unfolded in late 2013, statements by Swedish officials

---

297 Tomson.

298 Pieter Bevelander and Anders Hellström, "Pro-and Anti-Imigrant Mobilizations in Polarized Sweden," European Studies (Éditions de l'Université de Bruxelles, 2019), https://doi.org/10.26530/OAPEN_1005529.

299 Tomson, "The Rise of Sweden Democrats."

300 Bevelander and Hellström, "Pro-and Anti-Imigrant Mobilizations in Polarized Sweden."

301 Bevelander and Hellström.

302 Bevelander and Hellström.

303 Bevelander and Hellström.

excluded the use of military force but condemned Russian action.[304] In 2014, the little green men appeared in Crimea to seize critical sites, which changed Swedish thinking. With diplomatic statements yielding no effect whatsoever, Swedish defense officials considered broader strategy, for example, how it could even defend its outlying Baltic Sea islands like Götland Island.[305] Götland Island was strategically and tactically important for controlling naval traffic near the Swedish coasts' high population areas.[306] Conversations about whether Sweden should finally join NATO emerged.[307] Sweden solidified their commitment to support Ukrainian democracy because the Crimean independence referendum appeared more like a hybrid war than a legitimate popular mandate.[308] Therefore, the Crimean invasion was a lightbulb moment for Swedish policymakers in the post-Cold War era.

By 2018, the true extent of Russian involvement was undeniable, and Sweden was still unprepared. The notion of a Russian invasion of the Baltic states seemed credible enough to prompt two ideological shifts in defense policy.[309] First, conscription recommenced after a

304 Anna Kobierecka, "The Swedish Perception of European Security in the Light of the Crisis in Ukraine," International Studies. Interdisciplinary Political and Cultural Journal 18 (December 1, 2016), https://doi.org/10.1515/ipcj-2016-0012.
305 Kobierecka.
306 Michael M. Phillips and James Marson, "Russian Aggression Spurs Neighbors to Rebuild Defenses," Wall Street Journal, January 5, 2021, sec. World, https://www.wsj.com/articles/russian-aggression-spurs-neighbors-to-rebuild-de-fenses-11609859853.
307 Kobierecka, "The Swedish Perception of European Security in the Light of the Crisis in Ukraine."
308 Kobierecka.
309 Peter Apps, "Why Neutral, Peaceful Sweden Is Preparing for War," Reuters, May 30, 2018, sec. Commentary, https://www.reuters.com/article/us-apps-sweden-com-mentary-idUSKCN1IV27N.

seven-year hiatus.[310] Sweden's conscription pause created gapped military billets that were no longer tenable. Second, Sweden began distributing leaflets to the public concerning civil defense and self-help during an invasion.[311] With time, Swedish officials had some discussions concerning a military union with Finland, which received much public support within Finland but ultimately proved uneventful.[312] The Swedish government gave Ukraine financial aid and diplomatic support while condemning Russia, but has not entered any further defense alliances.[313] Since the invasion, Sweden has had to reckon with some difficult facts. Sweden could not resist Russia in a conflict. Sweden's reversal in its liberal immigration policy in the face of scrutiny shows they were not as altruistic as once thought. The policy mistakes of Sweden have benefitted far-right credibility with its willingness to close the borders and restart mandatory conscription.

C.   SWEDISH RIGHT-WING LANDSCAPE

The Swedish right-wing political organizations had steadily increased popularity due to immigration and defense since 2014–2015. Subsequently, the fringe far-right changed from neo-Nazi gangs harassing minorities to a more focused, politically engaged movement. Since 2014, the groups have had a reason to organize, militarize, and strategize toward electoral victories, using immigration much like Poland's PiS. SD was ready to seize the moment as an established party

---

310 Government Offices of Sweden, "Sweden Re-Activates Conscription," March 2, 2017, https://www.government.se/articles/2017/03/re-activation-of-enrolment-and-the-conscrip-tion/?TSPD_101_R0=0840bf68c4ab2000328a92d0d1645e49068cc53b8da71e01fd1 bd4e03eeb1975bdff72a5a49c7e68087dab295b143000b09cdb3fab38bfa63a20f43a88 593f1ac4f0191ad1153f68763b55970d97004e846131024b056ac8d02f9a8d23139dd2.
311 Apps, "Why Neutral, Peaceful Sweden Is Preparing for War."
312 Kobierecka, "The Swedish Perception of European Security in the Light of the Crisis in Ukraine."
313 Kobierecka.

with serious anti-immigrant credibility when the migration crisis hit Sweden.[314] By 2018, SD represented 17.5 percent of the vote, corresponding to 62 of the 349 seats in the Riksdag.[315] These seats came at the cost of the centrists, with the center-left Social Democrats, who lost 13 seats, and the center-right Moderates, lost 14 seats.[316] In parliament, SD pressured the other centrist parties to take on anti-immigrant policies to maintain vote share.[317] SD progression from a fringe party to a mainstream party was a monumental achievement for their movement.

SD was well placed among the parties to reinvigorate Swedish defense initiatives. Due to the uncertainty an irridentist Russia poses to the Baltic, a consensus was forming around defense policy among the major Swedish parties.[318] The 2018 election was the last to occur and each party advocated increases in defense spending from the then-historic low of 1.03 percent of gross domestic product to 2.2 percent over the next decade.[319] The SD webpage specifically advocated for an increase in infantry size from two brigades to seven brigades.[320] The website also called for a strengthened and expanded artillery corps. If SD is the pro-defense party, then further turmoil will benefit them more.

---

314 Tomson, "The Rise of Sweden Democrats."

315 Tomson.

316 Tomson.

317 Benjamin R. Teitelbaum, "In Sweden, Populist Nationalists Won on Policy, but Lost on Politics," The Atlantic, September 12, 2018, https://www.theatlantic.com/ideas/archive/2018/09/in-sweden-populist-nationalists-won-on-policy-but-lost-on-politics/569968/.

318 Gerard O'Dwyer, "New Swedish Government Advocates for Greater Defense Spending," Defense News, September 13, 2018, https://www.defensenews.com/global/europe/2018/09/12/new-swedish-government-advocates-for-greater-defense-spending/.

319 O'Dwyer.

320 Sweden Democrats, "A-Ö [A to Z]," Sverigedemokraterna (blog), accessed July 22, 2021, https://sd.se/a-o/.

But SD, like the other major parties, opposed NATO membership even as the option found new life in defense circles.[321] As recently as June 2021, NATO policy proposals came just as SD unseated the seven-year incumbent Prime Minister of Sweden.[322] SD's political calculus was a shrewd measure to consolidate its vote share by calling for new elections SD presumed would allocate them more Riksdag seats and therefore allow them to form the coalition government. SD has been making all the right moves in a political climate that trends rightwards in the last few years. SD posed a threat to the Swedish establishment. Unlike other populists in Europe, SD was a sort of king-maker party within Swedish politics due to its prescience on some critical issues without the illiberal aspects that bring condemnation which PiS often struggles. Therefore, SD could become a rubric for the far right to copy elsewhere.

While SD represented the far right's political instrument, the wider movement that supports them was getting more connected to the rest of Europe. One recent example was the connection between the Polish and Swedish far-right.[323] Members of a Swedish-based group called Nordic Youth made connections with the Polish far-right ONR.[324] The Nordic Youth was a schism organization whose leadership was deemed too white supremacist for their parent Sweden Nationalist Democrat Party. The Nordic Youth have since embraced SD

---

321 "Majority in Swedish Parliament Backs 'NATO Option' after Sweden Democrats Shift," Reuters, December 9, 2020, sec. 2020 Candidate Slideshows, https://www.reuters.com/article/sweden-nato-idUSKBN28J1UL.
322 "Sweden's PM Resigning, Calls for Parliament to Form New Govt," AP News, June 28, 2021, sec. Stefan Lofven, https://apnews.com/article/europe-government-and-politics-d7546553ae23468bbf73be5373068893.
323 "Polsk extremhöger aktiv i Sverige [Polish Far-Right Active in Sweden]," Bonnier News Local AB, February 9, 2016, https://www.dt.se/artikel/polsk-extremhoger-aktiv-i-sverige.
324 Bonnier News Local AB.

and found a common cause with ONR's tactics.[325] Likewise, Poles of ONR supported the Swedes' rallies and sometimes carried weapons at Stockholm marches.[326] The two groups have mutual targets in the immigrant population as well as the resurgent Russian threat.[327] The far-right crossover that is apparent suggests another inflection point for Swedish and other European far-right groups working together to exert their political will on a center-left dominated European political scene.

Though there were still many schisms among the European right; they tended to find foreign benefactors easily. In 2018, Sweden started its third-way party with Alternative for Sweden (AfS), connecting to Trump supporters in the United States for support.[328] This party rivals the SD because the founding members' expulsion from SD meant they had to free reign for their intense radicalism.[329] AfS party's website had crowdsourced funding from U.S. Trump supporters due to mutual fear of immigrant influxes and demographic change.[330] AfS seeks financial support to campaign against what AfS sees as political corruption, political correctness, and policies prompting a minority status of the Swedish people within their country.[331] The third-way in Sweden is not a powerful force, but its ability to attract foreign support makes them another threat to Swedish security.

---

325 Anders Dalsbro, "Med Skräcken Som Vapen [With Fear as a Weapon]," Expo.se, March 1, 2011, https://expo.se/2011/03/med-skr%C3%A4cken-som-vapen.

326 Bonnier News Local AB, "Polish Far-Right Active in Sweden."

327 Bonnier News Local AB.

328 Per Sefastsson, "Press Release: Alternative for Sweden Launches International Crowdfunding Campaign," Alternativ för Sverige, March 20, 2018, https://alternativforsverige.se/press-release-alternative-for-sweden-launches-international-crowdfunding-campaign/.

329 Jan Henrik Holst, "Die Situation in Schweden [The Situation in Sweden]," Tichys Einblick, May 26, 2018, http://www.tichyseinblick.de/gastbeitrag/die-situation-in-schweden/.

330 Sefastsson, "Press Release."

331 Sefastsson.

The Swedish far-right has stylized, if not invented, weaponized criminal statistics that have caught the attention of prominent political figures like Nigel Farage and Donald Trump.[332] Farage was best known as the architect/advocate for the Brexit vote to withdraw United Kingdom's membership from the EU. Farage's leadership of the United Kingdom Independence Party (UKIP), later the Brexit Party, aimed a withering critique of European immigration practices that most mainstream politicians could not dare explore.[333] For instance, Farage claimed that Sweden's third-largest city and home to a booming immigrant population, Malmö, had become the world's "rape capital," while President Trump commented that Sweden had lots of problems with the large numbers of immigrants.[334] These comments coincided with the perceived growth of no-go zones or vulnerable areas/risk areas in Sweden's poorest areas.[335] While police deny there were areas police could not patrol, a published list of 22 Swedish neighborhoods indicated otherwise. Some "special services" like police escorts for emergency responders entering certain areas or other services employed for the most hard-bitten criminal areas became emblematic of immigration in Sweden.[336] Crime in Sweden is fodder for far-right narratives that drive voters to the ballot box.

Since 2014, there has been a corresponding increase in violence between Swedes and immigrants that the far-right perpetuates and points to as proof of incompatibility. In 2014, an uptick in immigrant

---

332 "Reality Check: Is Malmö the 'Rape Capital' of Europe?," BBC News, February 24, 2017, https://www.bbc.com/news/uk-politics-39056786.
333 Rosie Goldsmith, "Profile: Nigel Farage, UKIP Leader," BBC News, December 4, 2012, https://www.bbc.com/news/uk-politics-20543513.
334 BBC News, "Reality Check."
335 Tomson, "The Rise of Sweden Democrats."
336 "Here's the New Police List of Trouble Suburbs in Sweden," Local Sweden, June 3, 2019, https://www.thelocal.se/20190603/sweden-vulnerable-areas-decrease-positive-trends-police/.

inflicted violence on Swedes emerged.[337] In 2016, the attacks led to counterattacks where masked gangs targeting immigrants were likely the work of Sweden's far-right groups.[338] Bomb attacks have been another recent problem associated with Sweden's newly formed criminal gangs.[339] Bombings were not tracked in Sweden before 2017, yet 2018 had 162, and in 2019 there were 97 counted at the time of reporting.[340] In its criminal statistics, Sweden does not track ethnicity but police believe many bombers are second-and third-generation immigrants from economically challenged areas.[341] Other examples used by the far-right as justifications are tensions surfacing from the 2020 Quran-burning event that turned into a riot in Malmö.[342] The Swedish far-right point out these instances but even well-meaning Swedes are beginning to understand the slow, laborious process society has to become a welcoming melting pot culture.

The Swedish far-right groups have begun to find common ground with the far-right abroad. What were nationalistic, insular right-wing camps are now internalizing some lessons from the ubiquitous progressive landscape: think globally, act locally. The internationalizing of Sweden's far-right presents more opportunities with internet communication. A Swedish extremist may now receive financial and moral support from the United States, weapons training in Poland or Russia, and then use the internet to further recruit across Europe to harass migrants from Asia.

---

337 Tomson, "The Rise of Sweden Democrats."
338 "Sweden Masked Gang 'Targeted Migrants' in Stockholm," BBC News, January 30, 2016, https://www.bbc.com/news/world-europe-35451080.
339 "Sweden's 100 Explosions This Year: What's Going On?," BBC News, November 12, 2019, https://www.bbc.com/news/world-europe-50339977.
340 BBC News.
341 BBC News.
342 "Protest against Koran-Burning Turns Violent in Sweden," BBC News, August 29, 2020, https://www.bbc.com/news/world-europe-53959492.

D.   SWEDISH PARAMILITARIES

Sweden's paramilitaries spanned the spectrum of behaviors, but a common tactic was vigilante patrols. One group serving this purpose was the Soldiers of Odin. The Soldiers of Odin were a relatively socially inclined group of people who gather to conduct night patrols of many Swedish cities for fear of immigrant crime.[343] They were analogous to a racist version of New York City's Guardian Angels. Their stated aim was to protect women and children at night from immigrants in the streets of Finland and Sweden.[344] Although they were a neo-Nazi group, they were understood to be less extreme than other groups because of their insistence on basic decorum and pro-social utilitarian purpose.[345] An article assessing the group's invitation-only Facebook page states ethnicity was not a factor for their protection.[346] Yet, the group is a haven for Nazi imagery and derogatory jokes.[347] The growth of vigilante groups provides another cause for concern in Sweden's security services.

The Soldiers were expanding their reach outside of Stockholm to include outlying Swedish towns like Uppsala.[348] The addition of

---

343 Anders Gustafson, "DT Granskar: Medborgargarde Vill Skydda FRån Brott - Flera Soldiers of Odin-Aktivister Dömda För Brott [DT Examines: Citizen Guard Wants to Protect from Crime - Several Soldiers of Odin Activists Convicted of Crime]," Dt.Se, March 25, 2016, https://www.dt.se/artikel/dt-granskar-medborgar-garde-vill-skydda-fran-brott-flera-soldiers-of-odin-aktivister-domda-for-brott.
344 Gustafson.
345 Gustafson.
346 "Soldiers of Odin's Secret Facebook Group: Weapons, Nazi Symbols and Links to MV Lehti," Yle Uutiset, May 17, 2017, https://web.ar-chive.org/web/20170517012354/http://yle.fi:80/uutiset/osasto/news/sol-diers_of_odins_secret_facebook_group_weapons_nazi_sym-bols_and_links_to_mv_lehti/8749308.
347 Yle Uutiset.
348 Kristoffer Olofsson, "Concerns About Patrolling Civic Guard in Uppsala," Up-sala Nya Tidning, March 31, 1916, https://unt.se/uppland/uppsala/oro-for-patrul-lerande-medborgargarde-i-uppsala-4176238.aspx.

moderate Swedes to their political cause focused attention on mass migration's detrimental aspects in the country. The generation and dissemination of fear toward the immigrant community is a trademark of the far-right that the larger, more moderate electorate internalizes its message to erode public acceptance and political will for those immigrant communities most in need.

A unique facet of Sweden's paramilitarism was its anti-immigrant maritime patrols, looking to stop migrants entering the country by sea.[349] National Future actively patrolled suspicious vessels transiting the Oresund strait between Copenhagen and Malmö, where the Swedish Coast Guard failed to stop all smuggling and undocumented migration.[350] National Future intends to counter the do-gooder Swedes assisting migrants' at sea arriving in Sweden.[351] The group is associated with the Soldiers of Odin in mission and membership.[352] National Future developed contacts in Denmark that tip them off to suspicious boats headed into Swedish waters suggesting apparent cooperation with the Danish far-right.[353] The Swedish Coast Guard downplayed National Future's role in usurping their duties by stating the group overestimated how many boats have been interdicted. The Coast Guard has not seen National Future or many immigrants on the waterways.[354] However, Malmö's special prosecutor insisted on a spike in illegal migrant smuggling from Denmark contradicts the Coast Guard.[355] National Future is competing directly with the Swedish Coast Guard, and

349 Ulf Andersson, "Swedish Migrant Hunters Who Call Themselves Pirates," Daily Mail, April 1, 2016, sec. News, https://www.dailymail.co.uk/news/article-3516388/EXCLUSIVE-country-patrol-Nationell-Framtid-PIRATE-migrant-hunters-patrol-North-Sea-SPEEDBOAT-stop-refugees-getting-Sweden-door.html.
350 Andersson.
351 Andersson.
352 Andersson.
353 Andersson.
354 Andersson.
355 355 Kacper Rekawek et al., Violent Right-Wing Extremism and Terrorism –

each immigrant found provides propaganda for the anti-immigrant cause. The fate of undocumented migrants intercepted by armed vigilantes on isolated waters vowing to protect their country with force is a humanitarian concern.

Sweden's primary paramilitary force was becoming one of the most dangerous in all Europe. NRM's origins grew out of the transnational White Aryan Resistance movement, with WAR's Swedish chapter's founder, Klas Lund, serving as NRM's leader for several years.[356] Klas Lund had many serious criminal convictions, including racially motivated murder, robbery, and various firearm violations.[357] NRM's goals were third-way politics. NRM wanted democracy eliminated and a Nazi ethnostate opposed to capitalism, communism, and liberal democracy in its place.[358] NRM fought non-European migration into Sweden and attacked racial minorities and political opponents on the Left in the Nordic countries.[359] The movement expanded into Finland, Norway, Denmark, and Iceland, in addition to its collaboration with groups in the United States.[360] The group was highly active on social media and other internet platforms for recruitment. It also used the internet to coordinate propaganda, tactics, and fundraising with like-

Transnational Connectivity, Definitions, Incidents, Structures and Countermeasures (Berlin, Germany: CEP, 2020). p 115.

356 Johan Apel Röstlund, "NMR Splits - Klas Lund Forms a New Nazi Group," Arbetaren (blog), January 19, 2021, https://www.arbetaren.se/2019/08/14/nmr-splittras-klas-lund-bildar-ny-nazistgrupp/.

357 Röstlund.

358 "'За Рассею Пострадать Хочу'. Почему в Швеции Судят Националиста Из СССР ["I Want to Suffer for Russ." Why Is a Nationalist from the USSR on Trial in Sweden?]," BBC News Русская служба, February 21, 2020, https://www.bbc.com/russian/features-51586850.

359 Counter Extremism Project, "Counter Extremism Project."

360 Petter West, Linus Lång, and Kaisu Jansson, "Vuodetut viestit paljastavat: Natsijärjestö PVL yritti kosiskella isoa yleisöä ja käänsi samalla selän kaikista radi-kaaleimmille seuraajilleen [Leaked Messages Reveal: Nazi Organization PVL Tried to Court the General Public While Turning its Back on its Most Radical Followers]," Yle Uutiset, September 22, 2020, https://yle.fi/uutiset/3-11288020.

minded groups across Europe and North America.[361] The following illustrates a 2017 NRM march in Gothenburg.

Figure 4.   A November 2017 NRM demonstration in Gothenburg.[362]

NRM had a more violent mode of operation than other Swedish far-right groups. NRM members practice martial arts geared for street fights, and their members receive instruction from the organization on how to handle various violent situations.[363] Authorities alleged the group was behind several attacks from 2010 onward. NRM was

361 Kacper Rekawek et al., Violent Right-Wing Extremism and Terrorism – Transnational Connectivity, Definitions, Incidents, Structures and Countermeasures (Berlin, Germany: CEP, 2020).
362 Carl Ridderstråle, Members of the Nordic Resistance Movement Demonstrate in Gothenburg, Sweden, on 30 September 2017., September 30, 2017, September 30, 2017, Own work, https://commons.wikimedia.org/wiki/File:Nordic_Resistance_Movement_demonstration_in_Gothenburg.jpg.
363 Counter Extremism Project, "Counter Extremism Project."

suspected in a Gothenburg bombing of a communist political forum, and a violent altercation at an Antifa rally in Stockholm.[364] Since 2019, NRM has been banned in Finland for being contrary to Finnish law.[365] NRM violence represents a new level of far-right extremism in the Nordic countries not seen since the Third Reich.

NRM members were suspected of training in the Russian *Partizan* paramilitary training camps and conducting war abroad.[366] One Swede who attended the training center was accused of a Gothenburg asylum center bombing in 2016.[367] The Swedish Council for Preventing Violent Extremism stated that "Russian state's support for domestic and foreign extremists meant that officials cannot exclude the possibility of a foreign power supporting the NRM to aggravate political polarization in Sweden."[368] Sweden's paramilitary members are fighting in some of the same battles as their continental counterparts. The Soufan center reports that about 25 Swedes have fought in Ukraine.[369] The International Center for Counter-Terrorism reports that 250–300 Swedes fought in Syria.[370] NRM's capacity for violence and political action makes them a challenge to the liberal democracy when Sweden's own elected parliamentary members support the NRM, patronize NRM's webstore, or pay NRM membership dues.[371] Therefore, NRM is the clear focal point for Sweden's violent paramilitarism.

---

364 Counter Extremism Project.
365 "Finnish Top Court Bans Finland's Main Neo-Nazi Group," AP News, September 22, 2020, sec. Finland, https://apnews.com/article/finland-archive-courts-959402562fc46f29ac4a7fbf21fa6615.
366 Robert Lansing Institute, "Combat Training for European Neo-Nazis in Russia."
367 Robert Lansing Institute.
368 Robert Lansing Institute.
369 Blazakis et al., "White Supremacy Extremism."
370 van Ginkel et al., "He Foreign Fighters Phenomenon in the European Union. Profiles, Threats & Policies."
371 Kacper Rekawek et al., Violent Right-Wing Extremism and Terrorism – Transnational Connectivity, Definitions, Incidents, Structures and Countermeasures (Berlin, Germany: CEP, 2020). p 110.

The Swedish case showed members considered too extreme for NRM, so a recent schism produced Nordic Strength (*Nordisk Styrka*). Nordic Strength began in 2019 when NRM's violence-oriented hardliners wanted to reform away its political action group with paramilitary characteristics to create a true fighting force.[372] Nordic Strength members were amassing weapons, conducting murders, military preparations for terrorism, but the group remained intensely secretive, save for Klas Lund's involvement.[373] Articles indicated that Lund was forced out of NRM suggesting a split in tactical outlook.[374] Nordic Strength focused on terrorism while NRM gravitated to political action, meaning NRM was attempting to broaden the tent of support for the movement in Sweden. If there was another terror attack on a mosque or synagogue, it will probably originate from Nordic Strength and its affiliates. But both are gaining recruits from the European turbulence caused by immigration and a general rise in political extremism.

The Swedish paramilitary case correlates with a shift in the Swedish vote by converting the center-right voter to populist-right voters. The implication is that Swedish exceptionalism struggles with what it means to be tolerant and inclusive when those virtues bring problems. The tolerance paradox in the Swedish case reveals that open-minded, liberal values once cherished are threatened by the far right.

---

372 Röstlund, "NMR Splits - Klas Lund Forms a New Nazi Group."

373 Anna Fröjd, "Nya nazistgruppens innersta krets – fälld för över 100 brott [The Inner Circle of the New Nazi Group - Convicted of over 100 Crimes]," Expo.se, August 20, 2019, https://expo.se/2019/08/nya-nazistgruppens-innersta-krets-%E2%80%93-f%C3%A4lld-f%C3%B6r-%C3%B6ver-100-brott.

374 Röstlund, "NMR Splits - Klas Lund Forms a New Nazi Group."

E.   SWEDISH RESPONSE TO PARAMILITARISM

Cynics point to the reversal of immigration policy as not consistent with Swedish exceptionalism when it swiftly retreats under scrutiny. Like much of Europe, Sweden struggles with the societal divides that Russia and the immigration crisis opens. The issue of domestic terrorism from the far-right falls to the Swedish government agencies. The Swedish Security Service is the primary internal counterterrorism and intelligence apparatus safeguarding Sweden with cooperation from the police departments.[375] The Swedish Security Service website acknowledges the far-right movements' threat to Swedish democracy through digitalization and globalization. The Security Service website addresses these problems as having foreign connections and hybrid war implications while specifically mentioning Russia and China as threats.[376] The website further states that Russia uses influence operations and attempts to increase polarization to destabilize society.[377] The Security Services specify 2019 as an important year for the far-right attracting more people to the movement.[378] The Security Services are the main agency supporting Sweden's immigration and anti-terror policy.

Sweden's response to Russian activity is a return to total defense by rebuilding its military might. In 2017, Sweden reactivated its gender-neutral national conscription effective 1 January 2018 due to the volunteer force shortages. In 2018, the Swedish Civil Contingencies Agency republished its 20-page "If Crisis or War Comes" pamphlet and distributed it to 4.8 million households to prepare the country for

---

375 Swedish Security Service, "Swedish Democracy Under Threat on Several Fronts," text, March 26, 2020, http://www.sakerhetspolisen.se/en/swedish-security-service/about-us/press-room/current-events/news/2020-03-26-swedish-democracy-under-threat-on-several-fronts.html.
376 Swedish Security Service.
377 Swedish Security Service.
378 Swedish Security Service.

possible invasion or crisis.[379] The document had continuity with similar documents dating back to WW II with emergency preparedness checklists or instructions to resist the foreign power. The 2018 version also includes what to do in case of information technology attack, misinformation, and other likely hybrid warfare gambits.[380] It makes clear, "In Sweden there is a duty to contribute to total defense. This means that everyone who lives here and is between 16 and 70 can be called up to assist in various ways in the event of the threat of war and war."[381] The pamphlet also states, "If Sweden is attacked by another country, we will never give up. All information to the effect that resistance is to cease is false."[382] Sweden's total defense concept, along with its ever-present neutrality, are a cornerstone to its military deterrence.

Sweden's military thought continues to evolve as it incorporates new concepts from the various European think tanks. In 2019, Sweden published its *Strategic Outlook 8*, which emphasized the non-military parts of total defense that the whole of government must address.[383] It continued to highlight the hybrid, grey-zone security challenges in Ukraine by Russia in addition to the destabilizing effects of migration, economic isolationism, and populism's impact on Sweden's status quo.[384] The *Outlook* document also recognizes Sweden itself is a

---

379 Myndigheten för samhällsskydd och beredskap [Swedish Civil Contingencies Agency], "Om Krisen Eller Kriget Kommer [Whether The Crisis or The War Is Coming]," accessed July 27, 2021, https://www.msb.se/sv/publikationer/om-krisen-eller-kriget-kommer/.

380 Myndigheten för samhällsskydd och beredskap [Swedish Civil Contingencies Agency].

381 Myndigheten för samhällsskydd och beredskap [Swedish Civil Contingencies Agency]. P 9.

382 Myndigheten för samhällsskydd och beredskap [Swedish Civil Contingencies Agency]. P 12.

383 Niklas Rossbach et al., "Strategic Outlook 8: Sweden´s Total Defence - Challenges and Opportunities" (Swedish Defence Research Agency, October 24, 2019), https://www.foi.se/en/foi/research/strategic-outlook.html.

384 Rossbach et al.

small state, dependent on free trade, and the rules-based order ensured by other states indicating instability in Germany would be problematic.[385] These observations mean Sweden must be self-reliant while integrated into Europe in the right balance.

Sweden has increased its military readiness in other ways aligned with its unique place in Europe. The Riksdag approved a 40-percent increase in military spending for the 2021–2025 period for a total of $11 billion.[386] By 2030, Sweden aims to have a 100,000-person military.[387] As of April 2021, Sweden's forces stand at 60,000 members.[388] Yet, Sweden is reluctant to join NATO, seeing its political room for maneuver independent of the NATO bloc as essential to its security.[389] In the current context, Sweden's non-alignment means its military will need to produce innovative solutions to remain top-tier without the mutual support of a major defense alliance.

Sweden has good relations with its neighbors, NATO members or otherwise, should an incursion take place.[390] The Nordic Defense Cooperation (NORDEFCO) has five Nordic states: Sweden, Iceland, Norway, Finland, and Denmark.[391] NORDEFCO is a voluntary framework for cost-sharing and joint capability development in air surveil-

---

385 Rossbach et al.

386 Sebastian Sprenger, "Sweden Clings to Its Non-NATO Status amid Substantial Defense Budget Boost," Defense News, April 8, 2021, sec. Europe, https://www.defensenews.com/global/europe/2021/04/08/sweden-clings-to-its-neutrality-amid-substantial-defense-budget-boost/.

387 Sprenger.

388 Sprenger.

389 Arctic Institute, "Small and Non-Aligned: Sweden's Strategic Posture in the Arctic (Part II)," September 4, 2020, https://www.thearcticinstitute.org/small-non-aligned-sweden-strategic-posture-arctic-part-ii/.

390 Arctic Institute.

391 "About NORDEFCO," accessed July 27, 2021, https://www.nordefco.org/the-basics-about-nordefco.

lance, cyber defense, ground anti-access area denial, artificial intelligence, and space security.[392] The Swedish defense system alone may be inadequate for the country's needs at the high end of warfare due to costs and efficiencies of scale. But NORDEFCO's existence suggests Sweden intends to look towards Scandinavia as a military bloc and political lobby.

Sweden's defense system seems to mix self-reliance through deterrence with NATO membership overtures when it suits Swedish interests. One could argue that Sweden is neither strong enough to credibly deter Russia, while at the same time, not being a NATO member makes it a target for Russia due to Sweden's setting as a bastion for European political norms. If Russia were to attack, Sweden's coastal cities would be an obvious target of opportunity to increase Russian largess in the Baltic region. Yet, Sweden's signal about possible NATO membership might be another deterrence tool when times are tense.

F.   DISCUSSION

The Swedish paramilitary case has a resemblance to Germany yet departs in significant ways. Both are liberal western democracies that prospered from a militarily integrated Europe during the Cold War. Both stood down their Cold War defense apparatus when it appeared they won the Cold War. Both made themselves available to migrants fleeing the War on Terror's warzones. But in Sweden, the long-discredited far-right has made substantial electoral inroads amid Russian geopolitical strategy and dubious EU immigration policies. In the decade leading up to these problems, SD shifted its appearance from the skinhead party to a clean-cut, suit-and-tie politics while maintaining

---

392 "NORDEFCO Capabilities," accessed July 27, 2021, https://www.nordefco.org/COPA-Capabilities2.

those earlier supporters.[393] SD was more than prepared to articulate the problems with mass migration and a defensive stand down in Swedish society.

In some ways, the much-lauded Swedish social welfare system lays the framework for SD to wedge the issue against the open border issue. SD and NRM are not the first to question the open borders versus welfare state debate, but they apply it to their context in a fiercely vocal, and nationalistic polemic. As a matter of fiscal policy, there is also some contradiction between social welfare spending and defense spending where government spending is a zero-sum game. Sweden's defense has optimized the two costly endeavors well for decades, but a more fatigued, subdued United States means the balance might need reevaluation in Stockholm. Sweden uses its Home Guard and political maneuvering rather than committing to NATO's raison d'etre. But are these shrewd moves around perpetual European pitfalls, or are they a naïve ploy to be exposed as folly when trouble emerges? Janowitz might suggest Sweden's accomplishments with their broad conscription and emergency preparedness are commendable societal militarization policies. Sweden's neutrality arguably puts their military thinkers in the pragmatist camp due to their need for sovereignty results in clear-thinking military policy.

Sweden's rearmament is consistent with European trends, but because it nominally stands alone, there might be some applicability for NATO members to rededicate themselves to a self-reliant strategy while hoping for neighborly cooperation. Sweden's balance must be perfect in perception and in practice for that deterrence to work. It means the NRM cohort not be allowed to carry the message that they

---

393 "Bakgrund: Bakom den demokratiska fasaden [Background: Behind the Democratic Facade]," Expo.se, April 19, 2003,
https://expo.se/arkivet/2003/04/bakgrund-bakom-den-demokratiska-fasaden.

stand for Swedishness at the expense of the military or political representatives in a possible era of political Balkanization. It seems that Sweden must work overtime to continue its status quo of non-alignment, open borders, and generosity, while Russia plots a far-right surge in the liberal, democratic land of plenty. A recent string of SD successes means the upcoming 2022 elections could see SD taking a larger share, which the governing coalition would no longer be able to exclude from policy formation. Stopping the far-right renaissance in Sweden means a more nuanced immigration policy, a continuation of defense readiness to include the paramilitaries for defense purposes, and closer alignment with NATO and European defense initiatives.

V. CONCLUSION

This thesis aims to explore the civil-military relationship in three states where a fundamental shift in paramilitarism has occurred to understand the changing nature of Europe. Each case examined the details of the paramilitary historical record within a geostrategic context, along with recent events, to understand which solutions promise the best efficacy. These events were a rise in right-wing populism, an immigration crisis, and Crimean invasion as catalysts for the reconsidered civil-military relationship. The resultant paramilitary cultures presented a simultaneous opportunity and concern. Whether a country should engage with its paramilitaries and how best to handle their nationalism has implications for the coming decade of European security. The paramilitary policy recommendations in this chapter provide academic insights into each state's context.

A.   CIVIL-MILITARY RELATIONSHIPS

The civil-military relationship deserves consideration because the politically motivated paramilitary's ability challenges the fundamental aspect of what a state is: a structure maintaining a monopoly on violence within a given territory. Civil-military relations also act as an independent variable in defense readiness, which informs follow-on paramilitary policy. Therefore, any conversation about civil-military relations must include the role of political ideology because it is a source of division within the democratic world. The policies of a democratic government tend to be more subdued and less extreme than any subset of the politically motivated paramilitary. Political compromises are needed to govern a polity, while a paramilitary hierarchy can be ruled by dictate. Likewise, the social mores of society are not aligned with its military because of their different objectives and pressures. But a correlation between paramilitarism and far-right politics could be a source of strength and resilience against a foreign foe.

Those who wield weapons to maintain a state's supremacy exhibit a concentration of martial aptitude that can be guided to pro-social purposes. The far-right, military-minded citizens might have a deference for national history, civic pride, and love for the culture that form a vital aspect of modern nation-state coherence. The military and paramilitary operate in an anti-liberal and anti-democratic fashion where individualism is suppressed. The prioritization of a hierarchy based on experience and skill opposes the egalitarian ethos of European democracy. One lesson of this thesis is that the last 100 years represent the nadir and zenith of right-wing political action leading to national triumphs as well as mass atrocity.

The German far-right legacy is now suspect because it enforced a totalitarian police state detached from the prior republic's constitutional constraints leading to genocide. In Poland, the far-right is a symbolic champion of nationhood during their centuries of occupation and self-liberation. In Sweden, the far-right is more ambiguous because it is neither a clear hero against the Nazi and Soviet hegemons nor was an overt villain engaged in the Holocaust. Each state must choose its future relationship with the far-right with those experiences in mind as military threats continue to emerge. An eclectic approach might be optimal given the circumstances. Some elements of liberal progress and some military elements military might best enable a vital space for a flourishing society. More specifically, some reconceptualization of paramilitaries under civilian leadership is needed.

The German civil-military case shows a robust far-right presence, which the government has tried to eradicate. The 2017 Albrecht affair, the 2020 dissolution of a KSK unit due to extremism, and the extremist problems in the Bundeswehr Reserve force suggest issues exist with the far-right in the German military. Correcting that problem exacts a cost on German military effectiveness in theory and possibly in practice. These problems could amplify distrust between the civilians and senior military. The situation in Germany reveals an inconvenient fact the civilians would prefer to avoid: the far-right is problematic, but as a bloc, the far-right trend toward military service at far higher rates than political leftists.

The prominence of conduct problems in the German defense system suggests a new approach is needed. Using Janowitz's concepts, the German approach is pragmatic, but pragmatic shortfalls may yield weakness in the Bundeswehr. A cautious but judicious absolutist approach to military affairs could result in a better command structure. If one could imagine a less active United States, a slowly dissolving NATO with less American commitment, and a reckless Russian state seeking opportunity before its demographic collapse, then German absolutism makes sense. The problem with German nationalism and absolutism is that it brings Germany full circle to their Prussian militarism that precipitated the arms race leading to WW I and possibly another round of European conflicts. It is conceivable that a new milieu of *realpolitik* 21st century Otto von Bismarck types might continue the societal convergence toward a military society while playing the political game at its highest level to avoid total war. The security dilemma in Germany's case is familiar due to its existence in the North European Plain without a non-European security guarantor. Improved civil-military relations would be imperative to German interests.

In many ways, the move toward absolutist militarism is apparent in Poland. Polish civil-military relations are well aligned between the military, civilian government, and society at the moment. Polish paramilitaries, the ruling PiS party, and citizenry have a common cause in resisting Russia under the socially conservative Polish government. The Polish case shows some Janowitzian traits of militarizing society through Polish integration of paramilitaries. Poland shows a far-right presence in the military ranks coming from wider society. The far-right paramilitarists are tolerated by civilian leadership because they are more ideologically aligned, and more integral to Polish defense. Polish history indicates it does not have the military might of Germany or Russia in a head-to-head fight, so it must be creative to ensure its future sovereignty. Its history suggests Poland's fate is tied to the two hegemons of Germany and Russia, so the pragmatism of the past might need reconsideration as Europe must become less reliant on NATO, and Russia faces an existential crisis. If Poland is to survive, it must not make the mistakes of weakness of the past. Poland must militarize and promote absolutists who impose a deterrent posture.

Polish paramilitary governance through the Passport system is a forward-thinking concept to further use the civilian population for a defense that differs from conventional conscription strategies common on the European continent. Because the paramilitaries are voluntary, they exhibit a uniquely liberal quality in a Polish state that shows otherwise illiberal trends. The idea is worth exploring in states like Germany or Sweden. A cause for concern remains the Pro-Russian, pan-Slavic variants of Polish paramilitarism. These need to be monitored for malignancy in the same way Germany must watch the far-right in its military. The modest successes of the PiS's far-right paramilitaries suggest that the Poles are comfortable enough with the far-right effort to better endow the defense effort and, thereby, Poland's autonomy in the region.

The Swedish civil-military relationship is growing complex as tensions mount on the continent. One source of tension originates from the Swedish ruling coalition distrusting its expanding far right while the country creeps rightward with each subsequent election. The Swedish Prime Minister's June 2021 vote of no confidence means change may be coming where established parties can no longer avoid a government with SD. What his means for their paramilitaries is not entirely clear since SD has no formal policy recommendations regarding the matter except policies aimed to increase military capability.

But the Swedish government is taking steps to militarize society and remain untethered to NATO. Further, the Swedish government makes no effort to integrate any controversial aspects of its paramilitary groups. Sweden's NRM is fascist and ethnonationalist, so it follows that there is little room for rehabilitation of the paramilitaries' members. Sweden instead pursues a total-war strategy where virtually every member of society must work to liberate the country in case of invasion. The Russian threat to the Baltics requires strategically minded, possibly absolutist generals working the problem. Therefore, the Janowitzian civil-military convergence must be reevaluated as Sweden's situation with Russia resembles total war instead of limited war. Sweden might also look to Poland for inspiration to create a paramilitary system alongside its civil defense apparatus. The following graphic depicts Janowitz's concepts on an axis for a hypothetical future without an American-backed NATO in Europe.

Finally, there are some universal best practices to upgrade the civil-military relationship. Ruth and Strachan suggest that political messaging can improve societal resilience.[394] By recognizing hybrid warfare is the insertion of political influence from secretive bad actors, democratic leaders can improve societal stability through engagement in sophisticated dialogue on the need for defense rather than cynical partisanship.[395] Matei and Halladay recommend transparency, accountability, and dialogue as essential to the iterative process between civilians and the military leadership striving for a workable balance.[396] Thus the civil-military relationship depends on mutual knowledge, institutions with effective techniques, and a dedication to democratic norms in the

---

394 Strachan and Harris, "The Utility of Military Force and Public Understanding in Today's Britain."
395 Strachan and Harris.
396 Matei and Halladay, "The Control-Effectiveness Framework of Civil–Military Relations."

military community.[397] Drawing from these examples and the broader literature, solutions abound for Europe's changing civil-military situation.

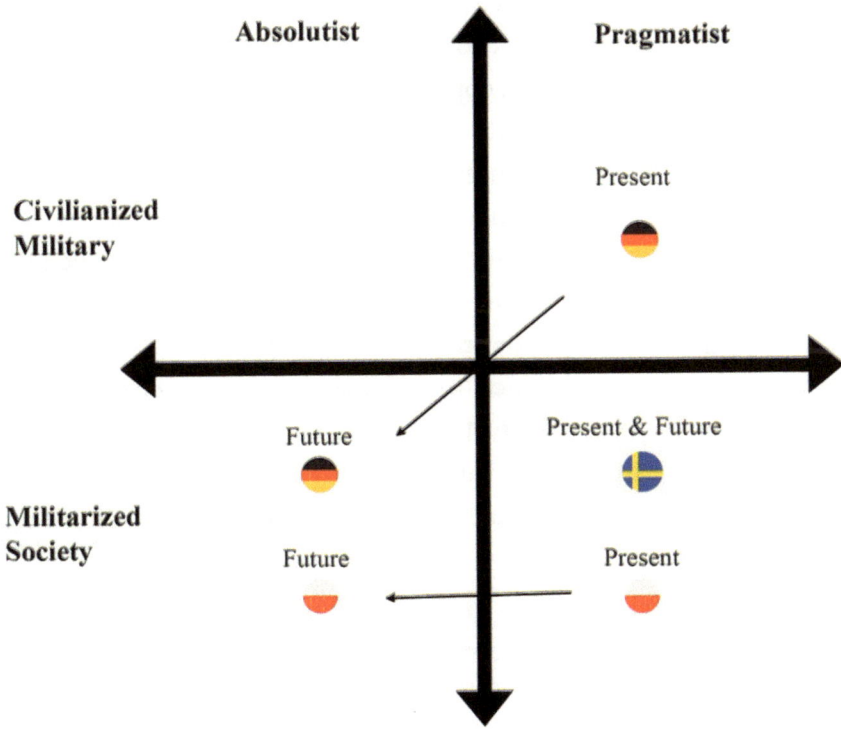

Figure 5. Janowitzian Axis for an imagined non-NATO future.

B.   PARAMILITARY POLICY

One problem the paramilitary cases show is their varying degrees of danger to the democratic institutions, but each has opportunities for improvement along with prospects for the advancement of civil

---

397 Matei and Halladay.

rights. The European states must make some demarcation and decisions to deal with the right-wing paramilitaries, as it is highly unlikely paramilitary forces can be eradicated completely. By understanding these three cases alongside the relevant research, a prudent policy can be implemented for an all-encompassing state strategy for paramilitary forces to serve the state's objectives. In particular, the paramilitary options must coincide with the geopolitical interests of contemporary Europe. These interests are the threat of hybrid war, a plausibly more isolationist United States, and surging right-wing politics in Europe. The three states have some rethinking to do on its core defense assumptions. Some of the relevant literature offers advice for the problems at hand. Namely, the suggestions are for paramilitaries to build locally, including paramilitaries in the state structure, make them accountable, and recognize they are political organizations from the beginning. Finally, even with these rules of thumb, the decisions still do not yield perfect policy. Instead of solutions, they offer tradeoffs.[398] These tradeoffs are where an informed elected official can make the most significant impact.

The German case has the most room for improvement in preventing the growth of malignant variants of paramilitarism while reinforcing potential sources of strength. The modern German state has reversed its historical stereotype where its predecessor state, Prussia, was thought to be an army that happened to have a state.[399] Currently, Germany is so far removed from its early martial culture that it could be considered a civilian state devoid of offensive capabilities.[400] If it chooses greater deterrence, then a paramilitary system along similar

---

398 Levan Ramishvili, Thomas Sowell: There Are No Solutions, Only Trade-Offs, accessed August 20, 2021, https://www.youtube.com/watch?v=3_EtIWmja-4.
399 Craig, The Politics of the Prussian Army, 1640-1945.
400 James J. Sheehan, Where Have All the Soldiers Gone?: The Transformation of Modern Europe (Mariner Books, 2009), https://www.amazon.com/Where-Have-Soldiers-Gone-Transformation/dp/0547086334.

lines as Poland is a prudent starting place. Building pro-government paramilitaries can be a force multiplier, adding multiple utilitarian functions to their defensive posture. If Germany is to undertake this, then it is imperative that Germany implements a semi-official model with high accountability for paramilitary leadership.

Gary Miller's research on principle-agency modeling suggests civilian control is enhanced by incentivizing paramilitary leaders who have superior knowledge on the state of military affairs toward positive outcomes.[401] Therefore, Carey and Mitchell argue that formal semi-official paramilitaries are superior to informal paramilitary structures for mutual goals, transparency, and accountability.[402] Their research also shows that semi-official variants are preferable when a strong state with high economic development exists.[403] The key takeaway is that the paramilitary leadership be accountable and have formal links to Germany's Ministry of Defense.

Another issue for Germany to solve is the paramilitary link to society, specifically at the local community level. Paramilitaries that serve and are based in a local community are more accountable, less predatory, and more under the control of democratic leaders.[404] One mechanism to bind the militia to the community is the identifiability of the member with social and economic ties to the community.[405] These community ties do not allow members to commit wrongdoing without suffering the consequences because they cannot leave the area of an offense.[406] It follows that any paramilitary structure built for deterrence

---

401 Miller, "The Political Evolution of Principal-Agent Models."
402 Carey and Mitchell, "Progovernment Militias."
403 Sabine C. Carey, Michael P. Colaresi, and Neil J. Mitchell, "Governments, Informal Links to Militias, and Accountability," Journal of Conflict Resolution 59, no. 5 (August 1, 2015): 850–76, https://doi.org/10.1177/0022002715576747.
404 Carey and Mitchell, "Progovernment Militias."
405 Carey and Mitchell.
406 Schuberth, "The Challenge of Community-Based Armed Groups."

by civilian leaders is best implemented locally and tied to the community it serves.

The issue of ideology produces another contentious issue for civilian authorities building up the paramilitaries. Political, ethnic, and religious cleavages are some of the motivating forces for paramilitary mobilization generally.[407] Some research suggests ethnically or politically based semi-official paramilitaries decrease the risk to state and civilian communities.[408] The political motives offer a tradeoff for Germans to consider; how comfortable would they be with far-right members joining these paramilitaries? Many would-be militia members would probably carry strong right-wing views into the military, so the delineation in pragmatic terms would be what's politically acceptable and legal. Overt Nazism and racism must be culled from the paramilitary ranks. Anti-government and revolutionary elements must be removed as well. Managing the political ideology of a paramilitary presents some problems with judgment calls and enforcement, seeing that the paramilitaries are not official militaries commanded by dictate. It might also be the case that the rejected paramilitaries join a more extremist group rather than cease efforts. A compassionate approach to the misguided offers some benefits, but all the observations regarding Germany apply to Poland and Sweden.

Poland needs to take greater control of its paramilitaries via the Ministry of Defense state-run structure. The Polish paramilitaries are not a centralized force but could become more militarily effective if they were. Kandrík suggests the state provide objectives, roles, and tasks for the Polish volunteers to increase the state leadership of its paramilitaries.[409] It also means that states administrate the manning, training, and equipping of the paramilitaries in Poland. The Territorial

---

407 Carey and Mitchell, "Progovernment Militias."
408 Carey and Mitchell.
409 Kandrík, "The Challenge of Paramilitarism in Central and Eastern Europe."

Defense Force (WOT) is an excellent initial effort, but the other paramilitaries still lack state support and leadership. Those other paramilitary groups could become a source of problems if the best and brightest are funneled into WOT while the others degenerate into pro-Russian, or criminal groups through a lack of supervision. Another way to increase Polish deterrent capability is the civil defense course discussions being had in Poland. The goal of these civil defense courses is to instruct college and high school students on military concepts. Since teaching martial skills to students is politically acceptable in Poland, those courses might be another line of effort to increase military knowledge in the countries' youth.

Sweden could align its far-right paramilitary groups to the state as well. As mentioned in the Sweden chapter, Sweden is host to a far-right, euro-skeptic renaissance to the detriment of its integrationist efforts. Combatting the isolationist and xenophobic far-right means some bargaining is necessary. Legitimation of some groups might allow some progress, given that the paramilitaries are state-led, state-supervised, and locally based. The groups that can work within those confines might be included in the civil defense structure. However, the state must recognize the reality of the situation that the paramilitaries come as they are. The paramilitaries are political and will go on being so. Where the line lays for the state is to be determined. It would make sense for the paramilitary members to maintain a clean criminal record like reservist forces to be eligible to serve. Sweden might also raise the civilian martial aptitude through education similar to Poland. On the other hand, if groups persist with criminal, anti-state behaviors, they could be pursued as terrorists and criminals via policing efforts. Ultimately, the paramilitaries can be a resource if well managed.

A controversial paramilitary policy recommendation worth discussing is the advancement of civil rights in civilian firearm ownership to increase defensive readiness through distributed militia capability.

Currently, the function of European paramilitaries requires some reflection on how defense can be facilitated in a worst-case scenario—an outright invasion or debilitating guerilla war. In those scenarios, enemy strategists would likely attempt to capture military installations hosting a paramilitary's arsenal in the early stages of conflict. However, there are currently legal blocks to the mass distribution of defensive firearms, such as the EU Firearm Directive 2017/853 also known as the EU Gun Ban, and other local laws.[410] The EU directive incentivizes member states to keep firearms out of civilian circulation with new semi-automatic weapons and magazine size restrictions.[411] If the EU could reconsider these restrictions, policies that increase firearm access could avoid the arsenal-bottleneck problem while adding a deterrent factor to would-be invaders.

There are precedents for gun ownership and pro-government militia in Europe. Readily accessible firearms are consistent with military patterns observed during Operation Gladio's anti-Soviet preparedness.[412] The Swiss Army relies upon a militia system with home-stored firearms and ammunition. The Czech Republic readily allows firearm permit issuance to its citizens.[413] The Czech Republic and the Baltic states also have Shall-issue concealed carry firearm permits meaning that if citizens ask for a license, the police shall issue one.[414] Finland has some of the highest per capita gun ownership in Europe, primarily due

---

410 "European Commission Strengthens Control of Firearms across the EU," Text, European Commission, accessed September 16, 2021, https://ec.europa.eu/commission/presscorner/detail/en/IP_15_6110.
411 "European Commission Strengthens Control of Firearms across the EU."
412 NATO's Secret Armies.
413 Zákony Pro Lidi, "Firearms and Ammunition (Arms Act)," Act No. 119/2002 Coll., accessed September 16, 2021, https://www.zakonyprolidi.cz/cs/2002-119.
414 "Guns in the Czech Republic — Firearms, Gun Law and Gun Control," GunPolicy.org, 2021, https://www.gunpolicy.org/firearms/region/czech-republic.

to its upland wild-game hunting.[415] Finally, Ukraine has no federal fire-arms statutes, but permit issuance is inconsistent, and many weapons are illegal due to their Donbas conflict procurement.[416] The simultane-ous European military retrenchment and rejection of liberal gun laws seems inconsistent given the Russian threat. The inconsistency is a par-adox where Europeans are eligible for military conscription, but most cannot easily own private defensive weapons given the looming threat.

Two striking patterns emerge from the firearms regulations throughout Europe. One pattern is that eastern European states tend to have more liberal gun laws. The liberal guns laws are possibly out of fear of Russian intervention or perhaps due to strong protection for wild-game hunting. The other pattern is the contrast between firearm ownership in Switzerland versus Ukraine. Both countries have a strong militia culture, but Ukraine lacks the institutional strength to support liberal gun rights, meaning strong institutions enable Swiss defensive power. These two observations suggest Europe's East might benefit from liberal gun laws supported by strong institutions.

C.   DISCUSSION

The paramilitaries will play an essential part in this future dy-namic and Central Europe's security dilemma. The success or failure of hybrid war as a strategy is partly determined by how paramilitary forces respond in the grey zone between war and peace. This thesis generally advocates the paramilitary developments, but any number of real-world concerns could change the paramilitary trajectory from a promising en-deavor to a fifth column. However, it is with some present caution that

---

415 Markku Sandell and Teemo Tebest, "Aseiden määrä Suomessa vähenee – katso, missä ovat maan 1,5 miljoonaa asetta [The Number of Weapons in Finland is Declin-ing - See Where The Country's 1.5 Million Weapons Are]," Yle Uutiset, accessed September 16, 2021, https://yle.fi/uutiset/3-8588611.
416 "Ukrainians Are Getting Armed," Warsaw Institute (blog), August 21, 2018, https://warsawinstitute.org/ukrainians-getting-armed/.

those building paramilitary resilience are wise to consider President John F. Kennedy's encapsulation of the situation in Cold War Europe, "We dare not tempt them with weakness. For only when our arms are sufficient beyond doubt can we be certain beyond doubt that they will never be employed."[417] The paramilitaries have a role to play in future European security.

417 John F. Kennedy, "Transcript of President John F. Kennedy's Inaugural Address," January 20, 1961, https://www.ourdocuments.gov/doc.php?flash=false&doc=91&page=transcript.

LIST OF REFERENCES

Abenheim, Donald. "Bundeswehr and Alternative Für Deutschland (AfD): 'Die Soldatenpartei'? [Bundeswehr and Alternative For Germany (AfD): 'The Soldiers Party'?]." In *Jahrbuch Innere Führung 2019*, edited by Uwe Hartmann and Claus von Rosen, 2019:392, 2019. https://www.bod.de/buchshop/jahrbuch-innere-fuehrung-2019-9783945861981.

Abenheim, Donald, and Carolyn Halladay. "Professional Soldiers and Citizens in Uniform: Some Thoughts on Innere Führung from a Transatlantic Perspective." Naval Post Graduate School, 2016. https://calhoun.nps.edu/bitstream/handle/10945/57113/Abenheim_Professional_Soldiers_and_Citizens_in_Uniform.pdf?sequence=1&isAllowed=y.

Abenheim, Donald, Carolyn Halladay, and Rachel Epstein. "Radicalization in the German Armed Forces and Beyond." Political Violence at a Glance, May 7, 2019. https://politicalviolenceataglance.org/2019/05/07/radicalization-in-the-german-armed-forces-and-beyond/.

Ahram, Ariel. *Proxy Warriors: The Rise and Fall of State-Sponsored Militias*. 1st edition. Stanford, Calif: Stanford Security Studies, 2011.

Andersson, Ulf. "Swedish Migrant Hunters Who Call Themselves Pirates." *Daily Mail*, April 1, 2016, sec. News. https://www.dailymail.co.uk/news/article-3516388/EXCLUSIVE-country-patrol-Nationell-Framtid-PIRATE-migrant-hunters-patrol-North-Sea-SPEEDBOAT-stop-refugees-getting-Sweden-door.html.

AP Archive. *Defence Secy Comments on Europe, France, Germany*. Video, 2003. https://www.youtube.com/watch?v=E0GnRJEPXn4.

AP News. "Finnish Top Court Bans Finland's Main Neo-Nazi Group." *AP News*, September 22, 2020, sec. Finland. https://ap-news.com/article/finland-archive-courts-959402562fc46f29ac4a7fbf21fa6615.

———. "Sweden's PM Resigning, Calls for Parliament to Form New Govt." *AP News*, June 28, 2021, sec. Stefan Lofven. https://ap-news.com/article/europe-government-and-politics-d7546553ae23468bbf73be5373068893.

Apps, Peter. "Why Neutral, Peaceful Sweden Is Preparing for War." *Reuters*, May 30, 2018, sec. Commentary. https://www.reuters.com/article/us-apps-sweden-commentary-idUSKCN1IV27N.

Arctic Institute. "Small and Non-Aligned: Sweden's Strategic Posture in the Arctic (Part II)," September 4, 2020. https://www.thearcticinstitute.org/small-non-aligned-sweden-strategic-posture-arctic-part-ii/.

Arimo, Reino. *Saksalaisten sotilaallinen toiminta Suomessa 1918 [German Military Action in Finland 1918]*. Rovaniemi: Northern Finnish Historical Soceity, 1991. https://www.amazon.com/Saksalaisten-sotilaallinen-toiminta-historica-septentrionalia/dp/9519617442.

Bachman, Bart. "Diminishing Solidarity: Polish Attitudes toward the European Migration and Refugee Crisis." *Migrationpolicy.Org* (blog), June 15, 2016. https://www.migrationpolicy.org/article/diminishing-solidarity-polish-attitudes-toward-european-migration-and-refugee-crisis.

Bapat, Navin A. "Understanding State Sponsorship of Militant Groups." *British Journal of Political Science* 42, no. 1 (2012): 1–29.

Bates, Robert H. *When Things Fell Apart: State Failure in Late-Century Africa*. Illustrated edition. New York: Cambridge University Press, 2008.

BBC News. "Migrant Crisis: Russia and Syria 'Weaponising' Migration." BBC News, March 2, 2016. https://www.bbc.com/news/world-europe-35706238.

———. "Poland and Baltics Feel Heat from Crimea." BBC News, March 12, 2014. https://www.bbc.com/news/world-europe-26526053.

———. "Protest against Koran-Burning Turns Violent in Sweden." BBC News, August 29, 2020. https://www.bbc.com/news/world-europe-53959492.

———. "Reality Check: Is Malmö the 'Rape Capital' of Europe?" BBC News, February 24, 2017. https://www.bbc.com/news/uk-politics-39056786.

———. "Sweden Masked Gang 'Targeted Migrants' in Stockholm." BBC News, January 30, 2016. https://www.bbc.com/news/world-europe-35451080.

———. "Sweden's 100 Explosions This Year: What's Going On?" BBC News, November 12, 2019. https://www.bbc.com/news/world-europe-50339977.

———. "The Right-Wing Nationalists Shaking Up Europe." BBC News, November 13, 2019. https://www.bbc.com/news/world-europe-36130006.

———. "Ukraine's Most-Feared Volunteers." BBC News, February 27, 2015. https://www.bbc.com/news/av/world-europe-31657354.

Beevor, Antony. *Berlin: The Downfall, 1945*. New Haven, CN: Penguin Books, Limited, 2010.

Bendersky, Joseph W. *A Concise History of Nazi Germany*. Fourth edition. Lanham: Rowman & Littlefield Publishers, 2013.

Bennhold, Katrin. "As Neo-Nazis Seed Military Ranks, Germany Confronts 'an Enemy Within' - The New York Times." *New York Times*, July 3, 2020. https://www.nytimes.com/2020/07/03/world/europe/germany-military-neo-nazis-ksk.html.

Bevelander, Pieter, and Anders Hellström. "Pro-and Anti-Imigrant Mobilizations in Polarized Sweden." European Studies. Éditions de l'Université de Bruxelles, 2019. https://doi.org/10.26530/OAPEN_1005529.

Biddiscombe, Perry. *The Last Nazis: SS Werewolf Guerrilla Resistance in Europe 1944-1947*. 1st Edition. Stroud: Tempus Pub Ltd, 2000.

Bideleux, Robert, and Ian Jeffries. *A History of Eastern Europe: Crisis and Change*. 1st edition. London ; New York: Routledge, 1998.

Bieber, Florian. "How Europe's Nationalists Became Internationalists." *Foreign Policy*, November 30, 2019. https://foreignpolicy.com/2019/11/30/how-europes-nationalists-became-internationalists/.

Bierbach, Mara. "AfD, CDU, SPD: Where Do German Parties Stand on Refugees, Asylum and Immigration?" *Deutsche Welle*, September 24, 2017. https://www.dw.com/en/afd-cdu-spd-where-do-german-parties-stand-on-refugees-asylum-and-immigration/a-40610988.

Blazakis, Jason, Janet Byrne, Colin P. Clarke, Mohamed H. El Shawesh, Stephanie Foggett, Arkadiusz Legieć, Christopher Maldonado, et al. "White Supremacy Extremism: The Transnational Rise of the Violent White Supremacist Movement." The Soufan Center, September. https://thesoufancenter.org/research/white-supremacy-extremism-the-transnational-rise-of-the-violent-white-supremacist-movement/.

Bonnier News Local AB. "Polsk extremhöger aktiv i Sverige [Polish Far-Right Active in Sweden]." *Bonnier News Local AB*, February 9, 2016. https://www.dt.se/artikel/polsk-extremhoger-aktiv-i-sverige.

Boros, Tamás, Maria Freitas, Tibor Kadlót, and Enrst Stetter. "The State of Populism in Europe." Foundation for European Progressive Studies, 2016.

Braunthal, Gerard. *Right-Wing Extremism in Contemporary Germany*. Basingstoke, UK: Palgrave Macmillan, 2009. https://doi.org/10.1057/9780230251168.

Broniatowski, Michał, and David M. Herszenhorn. "White Nationalists Call For Ethnic Purity at Polish Demonstration." *Politico*, November 12, 2017. https://www.politico.eu/article/white-nationalists-call-for-ethnic-purity-at-polish-independence-day-march/.

Bugaric, Bojan. "Europe's Nationalist Threat." *The American Prospect*, May 18, 2016. https://prospect.org/api/content/a08f230d-4c80-55cb-954e-7a76315ab26e/.

Bundeszentrale für Politische Bildung. "Handwörterbuch des politischen Systems der Bundesrepublik Deutschland [Concise Dictionary of the Political System of the Federal Republic of Germany]." In *Bundeszentrale für Politische Blidung*. Bundeszentrale für politische Bildung, 2021. https://www.bpb.de/nachschlagen/lexika/handwoerterbuch-politisches-system/.

Burack, Christina. "Germany: Over 500 Right-Wing Extremists Suspected in Bundeswehr." *Deutsche Welle*, January 26, 2020. https://www.dw.com/en/germany-over-500-right-wing-extremists-suspected-in-bundeswehr/a-52152558.

Bureau of Counterterrorism. "Country Reports on Terrorism 2019: Germany." United States Department of State, May 31, 2021. https://www.state.gov/reports/country-reports-on-terrorism-2019/germany/.

Callimachi, Rukmini. "ISIS Claims Responsibility, Calling Paris Attacks 'First of the Storm.'" *The New York Times*, November 14, 2015, sec. World. https://www.nytimes.com/2015/11/15/world/europe/isis-claims-responsibility-for-paris-attacks-calling-them-miracles.html.

Campbell, Bruce, and Arthur Brenner, eds. *Death Squads in Global Perspective: Murder with Deniability.* Palgrave Macmillan US, 2000. https://doi.org/10.1057/9780230108141.

Carey, Sabine C., Michael P. Colaresi, and Neil J. Mitchell. "Governments, Informal Links to Militias, and Accountability." *Journal of Conflict Resolution* 59, no. 5 (August 1, 2015): 850–76. https://doi.org/10.1177/0022002715576747.

Carey, Sabine C., and Neil J. Mitchell. "Progovernment Militias." *Annual Review of Political Science* 20, no. 1 (2017): 127–47. https://doi.org/10.1146/annurev-polisci-051915-045433.

Central Intelligence Agency. "Project: LCPROWL." Nazi War Crimes Disclosure Act. Washington, DC: Central Intelligence Agency, 2007. https://www.cia.gov/readingroom/docs/LCPROWL%20%20%20%20VOL.%201_0036.pdf.

Chivvis, Christopher. *Understanding Russian "Hybrid Warfare": And What Can Be Done About It.* Rand Corporation, 2017. https://doi.org/10.7249/CT468.

Chrisafis, Angelique, Peter Walker, and Ben Quinn. "Calais 'Jungle' Camp: Clashes as Authorities Demolish Homes." Guardian, March 7, 2016. https://web.archive.org/web/20160307205334/http://www.theguardian.com/world/2016/feb/29/french-authorities-begin-clearance-of-part-of-calais-jungle-camp.

Cieślikowa, Agnieszka. *Ochotnicza Legia Kobiet [Volunteer Legia Women]: 1918-1922*. Warszawa: Bellona, 1998. https://www.amazon.com/Ochotnicza-Legia-Kobiet-1918-1922-Polish/dp/8311088780.

Clausewitz, Carl von. *On War*. Translated by Michael Eliot Howard and Peter Paret. Revised ed. Edition. Princeton, N.J: Princeton University Press, 1989.

Cohen, Ben. "Fury over Polish Government's Appointment of Former Far Right '100% Aryan' Activist to Leading State Post." *Algemeiner.Com*, February 18, 2021. https://www.algemeiner.com/2021/02/18/fury-over-polish-governments-appointment-of-former-far-right-100-aryan-activist-to-leading-state-post/.

Counter Extremism Project. "Germany: Extremism and Terrorism." Counter Extremism Project, May 2021. https://www.counterextremism.com/countries/germany.

———. "Nordic Resistance Movement." Counter Extremism Project. Accessed July 26, 2021. https://www.counterextremism.com/supremacy/nordic-resistance-movement.

Craig, Gordon. *The Politics of the Prussian Army, 1640-1945*. 1st edition. Oxford University Press, 1956.

Croft, Adrian. "European Union Signs Landmark Association Agreement with Ukraine." *Reuters*, March 21, 2014. https://www.reuters.com/article/us-ukraine-crisis-eu-agreement-idUSBREA2K0JY20140321.

Curtis, Glenn E. *Poland: A Country Study*. Area Handbook Series. Library of Congress Federal Research Division. Accessed April 19, 2021. http://countrystudies.us/poland/15.htm.

Dalsbro, Anders. "Med Skräcken Som Vapen [With Fear as a Weapon]." *Expo.se*, March 1, 2011. https://expo.se/2011/03/med-skr%C3%A4cken-som-vapen.

Der Spiegel. "Für Ehrliche Zusammenarbeit [For Honest Cooperation]." *Der Spiegel*, May 8, 1994. https://www.spiegel.de/politik/fuer-ehrliche-zusammenarbeit-a-160581e0-0002-0001-0000-000013684238.

———. "Panzer Von Links [Tanks From The Left]." *Der Spiegel*, May 14, 1978. https://www.spiegel.de/politik/panzer-von-links-a-98db3653-0002-0001-0000-000040615444.

———. "Verbrecher Als Vorbilder? [Criminals as Role Models?]." *Der Spiegel*, February 25, 2007. https://www.spiegel.de/politik/verbrecher-als-vorbilder-a-e7cdec37-0002-0001-0000-000050666658.

Deutsche Welle. "German Population of Migrant Background Rises to 21 Million." *Deutsche Welle*, July 28, 2020. https://www.dw.com/en/german-population-of-migrant-background-rises-to-21-million/a-54356773.

———. "Germany Places Entire Far-Right AfD Under Surveillance." *Deutsche Welle*, March 3, 2021. https://www.dw.com/en/germany-places-entire-far-right-afd-under-surveillance-reports/a-56757489.

———. "New Twist in Case of Slain German Politician Walter Lübcke." *Deutsche Welle*, September 1, 2020. https://www.dw.com/en/new-twist-in-case-of-slain-german-politician-walter-l%C3%BCbcke/a-51935858.

Doomed Soldiers. "Anti-Communist Underground In Poland 1944-1963." Accessed May 3, 2021. http://www.doomedsoldiers.com/introduction.html.

Dörrbrecker, Maximillian. "European Migrant Crisis." In *Wikipedia*, October 1, 2021. https://en.wikipedia.org/w/index.php?title=European_migrant_crisis&oldid=1047564505.

Eckel, Mike. "A Cry from Crimea." *World Policy Journal* 31, no. 4 (2014): 85–96.

Ellyatt, Holly. "Germany's Far-Right AfD Party: 5 Things You Need to Know." CNBC, September 25, 2017. https://www.cnbc.com/2017/09/25/germany-far-right-afd-party-5-things-you-need-to-know.html.

Erb, Sebastian. "Rechtsextreme Netzwerke in Deutschland: Ein deutscher Soldat [Right-Wing Extremist Networks in Germany: A German Soldier]." *Die Tageszeitung*, May 16, 2021, sec. taz, society. https://taz.de/!5767295/.

European Neighbourhood Policy And Enlargement Negotiations - European Commission. "EU Conditions for Membership." Text, December 6, 2016. https://ec.europa.eu/neighbourhood-enlargement/policy/conditions-membership_en.

European Centre of Excellence for Countering Hybrid Threats. "What Is Hybrid CoE." Hybrid CoE - The European Centre of Excellence for Countering Hybrid Threats. Accessed May 27, 2021. https://www.hybridcoe.fi/who-what-and-how/.

European Commission. "European Commission Strengthens Control of Firearms across the EU." Text. Accessed September 16, 2021. https://ec.europa.eu/commission/presscorner/detail/en/IP_15_6110.

European Council on Foreign Relations. "A Majority of Europe's Voters Do Not Consider Migration to Be the Most Important Issue, According to Major New Poll." *European Council on Foreign Relations* (blog), April 1, 2019. https://ecfr.eu/article/european_voters_do_not_consider_migration_most_important_election/.

European Security Academy. "ESA - Home Page." European Security Academy, April 2021. https://www.euseca.com/.

Haaretz.com. "Ex-Hate Group Leader Tasked with Fighting Hate Speech in Poland, Jewish Group Says." Accessed July 9, 2021. https://www.haaretz.com/world-news/europe/ex-hate-group-leader-tasked-with-fighting-hate-speech-in-poland-jewish-group-says-1.6823492.

Expo.se. "Bakgrund: Bakom den demokratiska fasaden [Background: Behind the Democratic Facade]." *Expo.se*, April 19, 2003. https://expo.se/arkivet/2003/04/bakgrund-bakom-den-demo-kratiska-fasaden.

Falanga. "Dziesięć haseł polskiego falangizmu [10 Slogans of Polish Phalanxism]." *Xportal.pl* (blog), March 28, 2017. https://xportal.pl/?p=28865.

Federal Criminal Police Office. "BKA - Joint Extremism and Terrorism Defense Center (GETZ)." Accessed May 31, 2021. https://www.bka.de/DE/UnsereAufgaben/Kooperationen/GETZ/getz_node.html.

Federal Ministry of Defense. *2016 White Paper On German Security Policy and the Future of the Bundeswehr.* Berlin: Federal Ministry of Defense, 2016. https://issat.dcaf.ch/download/111704/2027268/ 2016%20White%20Paper.pdf.

Federal Office for the Protection of the Constitution. "Rechtsextremismus [Right-Wing Extremism]." Bundesamt für Verfassungsschutz. Accessed May 31, 2021. http://www.verfassungsschutz.de/DE/themen/rechtsextremismus/rechtsextremismus_node.html.

Federal Republic of Germany. Basic Law. Accessed May 12, 2021. https://www.bundesregierung.de/breg-en/chancellor/basic-law-470510.

Firearms United Network. "Tomasz W. Stępień, President of Firearms United, Delivered A Fiery Closing Remark." Accessed June 4, 2021. https://firearms-united.com/stepien/.

Flis, Daniel, and Anna Gielewska. "Pro-Defense Organizations Want Real Guns." *Vsquare.Org*, January 21, 2019. https://vsquare.org/pro-defense-organizations-want-real-guns/.

France-Presse Agence. "AFD Party Votes to Campaign for German Exit from EU." Guardian, January 13, 2019.
https://www.theguardian.com/world/2019/jan/13/afd-party-to-campaign-for-german-exit-from-european-union.

Fröjd, Anna. "Nya nazistgruppens innersta krets – fälld för över 100 brott [The Inner Circle of the New Nazi Group - Convicted of over 100 Crimes]." *Expo.se*, August 20, 2019.
https://expo.se/2019/08/nya-nazistgruppens-innersta-krets-%E2%80%93-f%C3%A4lld-f%C3%B6r-%C3%B6ver-100-brott.

Fürstenau, Mercel. "Meet Germany's 'Querdenker' COVID Protest Movement." *Deutsche Welle*, March 4, 2021. https://www.dw.com/en/meet-germanys-querdenker-covid-pro-test-movement/a-57049985.

Gazeta, Agencja. "Wyrok W Sprawie Przygotowania Zamachu NA Sejm: Brunon Kwiecień Skazany NA 13 Lat WIęZienia [The Verdict on the Preparation of the Attack on the Seym: Brunon Kwiecień Sentenced to 13 Years in Prison]." *Dziennik.pl*, December 21, 2015. https://wiadomosci.dziennik.pl/wydarzenia/artykuly/508750,jest-wyrok-w-sprawie-brunona-kwietnia-mezczyzna-skazany-na-13-lat-wiezienia.html.

Genscher, Hans-Deitrich. "1971 Bundesamt für Verfassungsschutz Verfassungsschutzbericht [Constitutional Protection Report 1971]." Accessed April 30, 2021. https://verfassungsschutzber-ichte.de/bund/1971?

Gerber, Theodore P. "Membership Benefits or Selection Effects? Why Former Communist Party Members Do Better in Post-Soviet Russia." *Social Science Research* 29, no. 1 (March 1, 2000): 25–50. https://doi.org/10.1006/ssre.1999.0651.

Gerwarth, Robert, and John Horne. *War in Peace: Paramilitary Violence in Europe after the Great War.* Reprint edition. Oxford: Oxford University Press, 2013.

Ginkel, Bibi van, Bérénice Boutin, Grégory Chauzal, Jessica Dorsey, Marjolein Jegerings, Christophe Paulussen, Johanna Pohl, Alastair Reed, and Sofia Zavagli. "He Foreign Fighters Phenomenon in the European Union. Profiles, Threats & Policies." Edited by Eva Entenmann. *Terrorism and Counter-Terrorism Studies*, April 1, 2016. https://doi.org/10.19165/2016.1.02.

Glińska, Paulina, and Magdalena Kowalska-Sendek. "WOT - Mission, Structure, Training," May 21, 2017. http://www.polska-zbrojna.pl/home/articleshow/22674?t=WOT-misja-struktura-szkolenie#.

Goldsmith, Rosie. "Profile: Nigel Farage, UKIP Leader." BBC News, December 4, 2012. https://www.bbc.com/news/uk-politics-20543513.

Gordon, Harold J. *Hitler and the Beer Hall Putsch.* 1st edition. Princeton, N.J: Princeton University Press, 1972.

Government Offices of Sweden. "Sweden Re-Activates Conscription," March 2, 2017. https://www.government.se/articles/2017/03/re-activation-of-enrolment-and-the-conscription/?TSPD_101_R0=0840bf68c4ab2000328a92d0d1645e49068cc53b8da71e01fd1bd4e03eeb1975bdff72a5a49c7e68087dab295b143000b09cdb3fab38bfa63a20f43a88593f1ac4f0191ad1153f68763b55970d97004e846131024b056ac8d02f9a8d23139dd2.

Gray, Randal, and Christopher Argyle. *Chronicle of the First World War: Volume II - 1917-1921.* New York: Facts on File Inc., New York, 1991.

Guardian. "Rightwing Law and Justice Party Wins Overall Majority in Polish Election," October 27, 2015. http://www.theguardian.com/world/2015/oct/27/poland-law-justice-party-wins-235-seats-can-govern-alone.

GunPolicy.org. "Guns in the Czech Republic — Firearms, Gun Law and Gun Control." GunPolicy.org, 2021. https://www.gunpolicy.org/firearms/region/czech-republic.

Gustafson, Anders. "DT Granskar: Medborgargarde Vill Skydda FRån Brott - Flera Soldiers of Odin-Aktivister Dömda För Brott [DT Examines: Citizen Guard Wants to Protect from Crime - Several Soldiers of Odin Activists Convicted of Crime]." *Dt.Se*, March 25, 2016. https://www.dt.se/artikel/dt-granskar-medborgargarde-vill-skydda-fran-brott-flera-soldiers-of-odin-aktivister-domda-for-brott.

Gzell, Tomasz. "Gowin: '4 listopada podczas kongresu Polski Razem zostanie zaprezentowana nowa formacja polityczna' [Gowin: 'On November 4, during the Polish Congress Together, a New Political Formation Will Be Presented']." *wPolityce.pl*, October 13, 2017. https://wpolityce.pl/polityka/362191-gowin-4-listopada-podczas-kongresu-polski-razem-zostanie-zaprezentowana-nowa-formacja-polityczna?strona=1.

Hacker, Andrew. "The Professional Soldier, by Morris Janowitz." *Commentary Magazine*, September 1, 1960. https://www.commentary.org/articles/andrew-hacker/the-professional-soldier-by-morris-janowitz/.

Harris, Geoff. *The Dark Side of Europe: The Extreme Right Today.* First Edition. Edinburgh: Edinburgh University Press, 1990.

Heinrich, Daniel. "SIPRI: Germany Significantly Increases Military Spending." *Deutsche Welle*, April 26, 2020. https://www.dw.com/en/sipri-germany-significantly-increases-military-spending/a-53250926.

Herbst, Jeffery. "War and the State in Africa." *International Security* 14, no. 4 (1990): 117–39.

Hockenos, Paul. "Poland and the Uncontrollable Fury of Europe's Far-Right." *The Atlantic*, November 15, 2017. https://www.theatlantic.com/international/archive/2017/11/europe-far-right-populist-nazi-poland/524559/.

Holmberg, Arita. "A Demilitarization Process under Challenge? The Example of Sweden." *Defence Studies* 15, no. 3 (July 3, 2015): 235–53. https://doi.org/10.1080/14702436.2015.1084174.

Holst, Jan Henrik. "Die Situation in Schweden [The Situation in Sweden]." *Tichys Einblick*, May 26, 2018. http://www.tichyseinblick.de/gastbeitrag/die-situation-in-schweden/.

Holzer, Jerzy. "The Political Right in Poland, 1918-39." *Journal of Contemporary History* 12, no. 3 (1977): 395–412.

Huntington, Samuel P. *The Soldier and the State: The Theory and Politics of Civil–Military Relations*. Revised edition. Cambridge, Mass: Belknap Press: An Imprint of Harvard University Press, 1981.

Janowitz, Morris. *The Professional Soldier: A Social and Political Portrait*. Re-issue edition. New York: Free Press, 2017.

Jegic, Denijal. "How East Germany Became a Stronghold of the Far Right." Accessed April 19, 2021. https://www.aljazeera.com/opinions/2018/9/29/how-east-germany-became-a-stronghold-of-the-far-right.

John Binkley. "Clausewitz and Subjective Civilian Control: An Analysis of Clausewitz's Views on the Role of the Military Advisor in the Development of National Policy." *Armed Forces & Society* 42, no. 2 (April 1, 2016): 251–75. https://doi.org/10.1177/0095327X15594450.

Jones, Mark. *Founding Weimar: Violence and the German Revolution of 1918–1919*. Cambridge, United Kingdom: Cambridge University Press, 2016.

Kamínski, Bartłomiej. *The Collapse of State Socialism: The Case of Poland*. Princeton University Press, 1991. https://www.jstor.org/stable/j.ctt7ztrrc.

Kandrík, Matej. "The Challenge of Paramilitarism in Central and Eastern Europe." German Marshall Fund of the United States, 2020. http://www.jstor.org/stable/resrep26757.

Karaszewski, Bogumił. *Partyzancka broń: O uzbrojeniu w Batalionach Chłopskich [Guerrilla Weapons: On Armament in the Peasant Battalions]*. Warszawa: People's Publishing Cooperative, 1980. https://www.amazon.com/Partyzancka-broń-uzbrojeniu-Batalionach-Chlopskich/dp/8320532019/ref=sr_1_1?dchild=1&keywords=Bogumił+Karaszewski&qid=1620063878&s=books&sr=1-1.

Kennedy, John F. "Transcript of President John F. Kennedy's Inaugural Address," January 20, 1961. https://www.ourdocuments.gov/doc.php?flash=false&doc=91&page=transcript.

Kershaw, Ian. *To Hell and Back: Europe 1914-1949 (The Penguin History of Europe)*. Penguin Books, 2016. https://www.amazon.com/Hell-Back-1914-1949-Penguin-History/dp/0143109928.

Knight, Ben. "The Rise of the Far-Right in the East." *Deutsche Welle*, September 21, 2010. https://www.dw.com/en/the-rise-of-the-far-right-in-the-east/a-5996369.

Kobierecka, Anna. "The Swedish Perception of European Security in the Light of the Crisis in Ukraine." *International Studies. Interdisciplinary Political and Cultural Journal* 18 (December 1, 2016). https://doi.org/10.1515/ipcj-2016-0012.

Koehler, Daniel. *Right-Wing Terrorism in the 21st Century: The 'National Socialist Underground' and the History of Terror from the Far-Right in Germany.* 1st edition. London New York: Routledge, 2018.

Lange, Philipp. "Total Defence: How Germany Should Implement A Whole-of-Government National and Collective Defence." German Federal Academy for Security Policy, January 2, 2018. https://www.baks.bund.de/en/working-papers/2018/total-defence-how-germany-should-implement-a-whole-of-government-national-and.

Lees, Charles. "The 'Alternative for Germany': The Rise of Right-Wing Populism at the Heart of Europe:" *Politics*, June 4, 2018. https://doi.org/10.1177/0263395718777718.

Lenz, Leonhard. *Demonstration von Wir Für Deutschland Am 3. Oktober 2019 in Berlin [Demonstration by Wir Für Deutschland on October 3, 2019 in Berlin].* October 3, 2019. Own work. https://commons.wikimedia.org/wiki/File:Demonstration_of_Wir_f%C3%BCr_Deutschland_2019-10-03_15.jpg.

Leslie, Roy Francis, ed. *History of Poland since 1863.* Cambridge ; New York: Cambridge University Press, 1983.

Leszczynski, Adam. "How the NSZ Fought: Attempts to Cooperate with the Germans, Robberies, Attacks on the Home Army." *OKO Press*, September 24, 2017. https://oko.press/walczylo-nsz-wspolpraca-niemcami-rabunki-ataki-ak-publikujemy-dokumenty/.

Lithuania Tribune. "Lithuanian and Polish Presidents Call For NATO Treaty Article 4 Consultations." *Lithuania Tribune*, March 7, 2014. https://web.archive.org/web/20140307142447/http://www.lithuaniatribune.com/64476/lithuanian-polish-presidents-call-for-nato-treaty-article-4-consultations-201464476/.

Local. "Here's the New Police List of Trouble Suburbs in Sweden." *Local Sweden*, June 3, 2019. https://www.thelocal.se/20190603/sweden-vulnerable-areas-decrease-positive-trends-police/.

———. "'Toxic Leadership Culture': Germany Shakes Up Elite Army Force Over Far-Right Links." *Local Germany*, June 30, 2020. https://www.thelocal.de/20200630/germany-to-partly-dissolve-elite-force-over-far-right-links-minister/.

Lodenius, Anna-Lena. *Extremhögern [The Far Right]*. Stockholm: University Press, 1991.

Lööw, Heléne. *Nazismen I Sverige 1924 1979: Pionjarerna, Partierna, Propagandan [Nazism in Sweden 1924 1979: The Pioneers, The Parties, Propaganda]*. Stockholm: Ordfront, 2004.

MAD. "Der Militärische Abschirmdienst [The Military Counterintelligence]." Accessed May 31, 2021. https://www.bundeswehr.de/de/organisation/weitere-bmvg-dienststellen/mad-bundesamt-fuer-den-militaerischen-abschirmdienst.

Manthe, Barbara. "On the Pathway to Violence: West German Right-Wing Terrorism in the 1970s." *Terrorism and Political Violence* 33, no. 1 (January 2, 2021): 49–70. https://doi.org/10.1080/09546553.2018.1520701.

Matei, Florina Cristiana, and Carolyn Halladay. "The Control-Effectiveness Framework of Civil–Military Relations." *Oxford Research Encyclopedia of Politics*, February 23, 2021. https://doi.org/10.1093/acrefore/9780190228637.013.1874.

McNeill, William. *History of Western Civilization: A Handbook*. University of Chicago Press. Accessed August 10, 2021. https://www.amazon.com/History-Western-Civilization-William-McNeill/dp/0226561607/ref=asc_df_0226561607/?tag=hyprod-20&linkCode=df0&hvadid=241953224058&hvpos=&hvnetw=g&hvrand=3941434626762747878&hvpone=&hvptwo=&hvqmt=&hvdev=c&hvdvcmdl=&hvlocint=&hvlocphy=9031899&hvtargid=pla-489122852321&psc=1.

Miller, Gary J. "The Political Evolution of Principal-Agent Models." *Annual Review of Political Science* 8, no. 1 (June 15, 2005): 203–25. https://doi.org/10.1146/annurev.polisci.8.082103.104840.

Ministry of National Defense. "Territorial Defense Forces." Ministry of National Defense. Accessed June 3, 2021. https://www.gov.pl/web/national-defence/territorial-defence-forces.

Ministry of National Defence. "Missions." Accessed July 7, 2021. https://www.gov.pl/web/national-defence/missions.

Moldovan, Anton-Gabriel. "Poland's National Security Policy in a New Regional Security Environment. Case Study: National Security Strategy of Poland (2014)." *Toruńskie Studia Międzynarodowe* 1, no. 11 (2018): 89–102.

Molotov, Vyacheslav, and Joachim von Ribbentrop. "Molotov-Ribbentrop Pact." Fordham University, August 23, 1939. https://sourcebooks.fordham.edu/mod/1939pact.asp.

Myers, Steven Lee, and Ellen Barry. "Putin Reclaims Crimea for Russia and Bitterly Denounces the West." *New York Times*, March 18, 2014, sec. World. https://www.nytimes.com/2014/03/19/world/europe/ukraine.html.

Myndigheten för samhällsskydd och beredskap [Swedish Civil Contingencies Agency]. "Om Krisen Eller Kriget Kommer [Whether The Crisis or The War Is Coming]." Accessed July 27, 2021. https://www.msb.se/sv/publikationer/om-krisen-eller-kriget-kommer/.

National Rebirth of Poland. "Brunon April - Present!" *Narodowe Odrodzenie Polski (NOP) – Nacjonalistyczna Opozycja* (blog). Accessed June 5, 2021. https://www.nop.org.pl/2020/08/06/brunon-kwiecien-obecny/.

NATO. "Joint Intelligence and Security (JIS) Division." NATO. Accessed May 27, 2021. http://www.nato.int/cps/en/natolive/107942.htm.

———. "NATO's New Spearhead Force Conducts First Exercise." NATO. Accessed July 8, 2021. http://www.nato.int/cps/en/natohq/news_118667.htm.

———. "NATO's Response to Hybrid Threats." NATO. Accessed May 27, 2021. http://www.nato.int/cps/en/natohq/topics_156338.htm.

———. "Readiness Action Plan." NATO. Accessed May 27, 2021. http://www.nato.int/cps/en/natohq/topics_119353.htm.

———. "Statement to the Media by the NATO Secretary General at the Press Conference Held at NATO HQ, Brussels after the Meeting of the NATO-Ukraine Commission." NATO. Accessed July 20, 2021. http://www.nato.int/cps/en/natohq/opinions_107682.htm.

NATO's Secret Armies : Operation Gladio and Terrorism in Western Europe. Routledge, 2005. https://doi.org/10.4324/9780203017777.

Neue Westfälische. "Bielefelder Rechtsextreme unterwandern Reservisten der Bundeswehr [Bielefeld Right-Wing Extremists Infiltrate Bundeswehr Reservists]." *Neue Westfälische*. May 2, 2021. https://www.nw.de/lokal/bielefeld/mitte/22948818_Bielefelder-Rechtsextreme-unterwandern-Reservisten-der-Bundeswehr.html.

Nordic Defense Cooperation. "About NORDEFCO." Accessed July 27, 2021. https://www.nordefco.org/the-basics-about-nordefco.

———. "NORDEFCO Capabilities." Accessed July 27, 2021. https://www.nordefco.org/COPA-Capabilities2.

Obóz Narodowo-Radykalny. "ONR Deklaracja Ideowa [ONR Ideological Declaration]." Obóz Narodowo-Radykalny. Accessed April 19, 2021. https://www.onr.com.pl/deklaracja-ideowa/.

O'Dwyer, Gerard. "New Swedish Government Advocates for Greater Defense Spending." Defense News, September 13, 2018. https://www.defensenews.com/global/europe/2018/09/12/new-swedish-government-advocates-for-greater-defense-spending/.

OECD. "Indicators of Integration 2012 - Sweden." Accessed August 3, 2021. https://www.oecd.org/migration/integration-indicators-2012/keyindicatorsbycountry/name,218347,en.htm.

Olofsson, Kristoffer. "Concerns About Patrolling Civic Guard in Uppsala." *Upsala Nya Tidning*, March 31, 1916. https://unt.se/uppland/uppsala/oro-for-patrullerande-medborgargarde-i-uppsala-4176238.aspx.

Onet Wiadomości. "Jarosław Kaczyński zapowiedziany jako Naczelnik Państwa [Jarosław Kaczyński Announced as the Head of State}." *Onet Wiadomości*, 45:56 100AD. https://wiadomosci.onet.pl/kraj/jaroslaw-kaczynski-zapowiedziany-jako-naczelnik-panstwa/jvest9.

Osęka, Piotr. "Jak ORMO czuwało [How ORMO Was Watching]." *Polityka*, February 19, 2011. https://www.polityka.pl/tygodnikpolityka/historia/1513094,1,jak-ormo-czuwalo.read.

Ostow, Robin. "Ne Art Bürgerwehr in Form von Skins [NE Kind of Vigilante Group in the Form of Skins]: Young Germans on the Streets in the Eastern and Western States of the Federal Republic." *New German Critique*, no. 64 (1995): 87–103.

Paczkowski, Andrzej, and Malcolm Byrne. *From Solidarity to Martial Law: The Polish Crisis of 1980–1981.* Central European University Press, 2007.

Palmer, Edith. "Firearms-Control Legislation and Policy: Germany." Web page. Law Library of Congress. Accessed April 19, 2021. https://www.loc.gov/law/help/firearms-control/germany.php.

Pankowski, Rafal. "Right-Wing Extremism in Poland." International Policy Analysis. Bonn: Friedrich Ebert Foundation, October 2012. https://library.fes.de/pdf-files/id-moe/09409-20121029.pdf.

Parallel History Project on Cooperative Security. "NATO's Secret Armies: Chronology." *Secret Warfare: Operation Gladio and NATO's Stay-Behind Armies* (blog), February 2021. http://www.php.isn.ethz.ch/lory1.ethz.ch/collections/coll_gladio/chronology76c1.html?navinfo=15301.

Pedrick, Clare. "CIA Organized Secret Army In Western Europe." *Washington Post*, November 14, 1990. https://www.washingtonpost.com/archive/politics/1990/11/14/cia-organized-secret-army-in-western-europe/e0305101-97b9-4494-bc18-d89f42497d85/.

Pereira, Anthony. "Armed Forces, Coercive Monopolies, and Changing Patterns of State Formation and Violence," January 1, 2003, 387–408. https://doi.org/10.1017/CBO9780511510038.016.

Petter West, Linus Lång, and Kaisu Jansson. "Vuodetut viestit paljastavat: Natsijärjestö PVL yritti kosiskella isoa yleisöä ja käänsi samalla selän kaikista radikaaleimmille seuraajilleen [Leaked Messages Reveal: Nazi Organization PVL Tried to Court the General Public While Turning its Back on its Most Radical Followers]." *Yle Uutiset*, September 22, 2020. https://yle.fi/uutiset/3-11288020.

Phillips, Michael M., and James Marson. "Russian Aggression Spurs Neighbors to Rebuild Defenses." *Wall Street Journal*. January 5, 2021, sec. World. https://www.wsj.com/articles/russian-aggression-spurs-neighbors-to-rebuild-defenses-11609859853.

Pifer, Steven. "Five Years after Crimea's Illegal Annexation, the Issue Is No Closer to Resolution." *Brookings* (blog), March 18, 2019. https://www.brookings.edu/blog/order-from-chaos/2019/03/18/five-years-after-crimeas-illegal-annexation-the-issue-is-no-closer-to-resolution/.

Poe, Ted. Congressional Record on the Russian Invasion of Crimea, Pub. L. No. 163 Cong Rec H 2091, H2091 (2017). https://congressional-proquest-com.libproxy.nps.edu/congressional/result/congressional/congdocumentview?accountid=12702&groupid=100340&parmId=1793369AAF1.

Polish Ministry of Foreign Affairs. "MFA Statement on the Sixth Anniversary of Russia's Annexation of Crimea." Ministry of Foreign Affairs Republic of Poland, March 16, 2020. https://www.gov.pl/web/diplomacy/mfa-statement-on-the-sixth-anniversary-of-russias-annexation-of-crimea.

Polska Times. "Fala Uchodźców? Statystyki Studzą Emocje [A Wave of Refugees? Statistics Cool Down Emotions]." *Polska Times*, September 25, 2015. https://polskatimes.pl/fala-uchodzcow-statystyki-studza-emocje/ar/8180618.

Poohl, Daniel. "Nordiska rikspartiet (NRP) [Nordic National Party (NRP)]." *Expo.se*, March 7, 2019.
https://expo.se/fakta/wiki/nordiska-rikspartiet-nrp.

Poushter, Jacob. "European Opinions of the Refugee Crisis in 5 Charts." Pew Research Center, September 16, 2016. https://www.pewresearch.org/fact-tank/2016/09/16/european-opinions-of-the-refugee-crisis-in-5-charts/.

Pudelek. *Dumny Morawiecki Przechadza Się Po Sklepie z Odzieżą Patriotyczną [The Proud Morawiecki Strolls Through The Patriotic Clothing Store]*. Poland, 2018. https://www.youtube.com/watch?v=8yRnmH4UVgM.

PWN Encyclopedia. "Freedom and Independence Association." Accessed May 3, 2021. https://encyklopedia.pwn.pl/haslo/;4002133.

Radio Poland. "New Polish Conservative Party Launched." Polskie Radio dla Zagranicy, March 26, 2012. http://archiwum.the-news.pl/1/9/Artykul/94458,New-Polish-conservative-party-launched.

Ramishvili, Levan. *Thomas Sowell: There Are No Solutions, Only Trade-Offs*. Accessed August 20, 2021.
https://www.youtube.com/watch?v=3_EtIWmja-4.

Reuters. "Germany Replaces Military Intelligence Boss after Far-Right Scandals." *Reuters*, September 24, 2020. https://www.reuters.com/article/us-germany-military-farright-idUSKCN26F2ZJ.

———. "Majority in Swedish Parliament Backs 'NATO Option' after Sweden Democrats Shift." *Reuters*, December 9, 2020, sec. 2020 Candidate Slideshows. https://www.reuters.com/article/sweden-nato-idUSKBN28J1UL.

Ridderstråle, Carl. *Members of the Nordic Resistance Movement Demonstrate in Gothenburg, Sweden, on 30 September 2017*. September 30, 2017. Own work. https://commons.wikimedia.org/wiki/File:Nordic_Resistance_Movement_demonstration_in_Gothenburg.jpg.

Robert Lansing Institute. "Combat Training for European Neo-Nazis in Russia." *Robert Lansing Institute* (blog), June 9, 2020. https://lansinginstitute.org/2020/06/09/combat-training-for-european-neo-nazis-in-russia/.

Röpke, Andrea, and Andreas Speit. *Blut und Ehre: Geschichte und Gegenwart Rechter Gewalt in Deutschland [Blood and Honor: Past and Present of Right-Wing Violence in Germany]*. Ch. Links Verlag, 2013.

Rossbach, Niklas, Josefin Öhrn-Lundin, Daniel Jonsson, Anna Sundberg, Sofia Olsson, Jakob Gustafsson, and Camilla Trane. "Strategic Outlook 8: Sweden´s Total Defence - Challenges and Opportunities." Swedish Defence Research Agency, October 24, 2019. https://www.foi.se/en/foi/research/strategic-outlook.html.

Röstlund, Johan Apel. "NMR Splits - Klas Lund Forms a New Nazi Group." *Arbetaren* (blog), January 19, 2021. https://www.arbetaren.se/2019/08/14/nmr-splittras-klas-lund-bildar-ny-nazist-grupp/.

Rothschild, Joseph. *Pilsudski's Coup D'etat*. East Central European Studies of Columbia University. Columbia University Press, 1966.

Sabine C. Carey and Neil J. Mitchell. "Progovernment Militias." *Annual Review of Political Science* Vol. 20 (May 2017): 127–47.

Sandell, Markku, and Teemo Tebest. "Aseiden määrä Suomessa vähenee – katso, missä ovat maan 1,5 miljoonaa asetta [The Number of Weapons in Finland is Declining - See Where The Country's 1.5 Million Weapons Are]." *Yle Uutiset*. Accessed September 16, 2021. https://yle.fi/uutiset/3-8588611.

Schuberth, Moritz. "The Challenge of Community-Based Armed Groups: Towards a Conceptualization of Militias, Gangs, and Vigilantes." *Contemporary Security Policy* 36, no. 2 (May 4, 2015): 296–320. https://doi.org/10.1080/13523260.2015.1061756.

Schwarzgruber, Małgorzata. "The Federation of Pro-Defense Organizations Was Established," March 21, 2015. http://www.polska-zbrojna.pl/home/articleshow/15466?t=Powstala-Federacja-Organizacji-Proobronnych#.

Sefastsson, Per. "Press Release: Alternative for Sweden Launches International Crowdfunding Campaign." Alternativ för Sverige, March 20, 2018. https://alternativforsverige.se/press-release-alternative-for-sweden-launches-international-crowdfunding-campaign/.

Sheehan, James J. *Where Have All the Soldiers Gone?: The Transformation of Modern Europe.* Mariner Books, 2009. https://www.amazon.com/Where-Have-Soldiers-Gone-Transformation/dp/0547086334.

Siemens, Daniel. *Stormtroopers: A New History of Hitler's Brownshirts.* Yale University Press, 2017.

Sieradzka, Monika. "Smolensk: The Tragedy That Defined Polish Politics." *Deutsche Welle*, October 4, 2018. https://www.dw.com/en/smolensk-the-tragedy-that-defined-polish-politics/a-43328611.

Silar. *WOT-Soldaten, Karpatenvorland-Brigade [WOT Soldiers, Subcarpathian Brigade].* September 24, 2017. Own work. https://commons.wikimedia.org/wiki/File:02017_0074_Karpatenvorland-WOT-Brigade.jpg.

Soshnikov, Andrey. "'За Рассею Пострадать Хочу'. Почему в Швеции Судят Националиста Из СССР ["I Want to Suffer for Russ." Why Is a Nationalist from the USSR on Trial in Sweden?]." BBC News Русская служба, February 21, 2020. https://www.bbc.com/russian/features-51586850.

Śpiewak, Jan. "Jarosław Kaczyński, Czyli Naczelnik Naszych Czasów - Ranking Najbardziej Wpływowych [Jarosław Kaczyński, The Chief of Our Time - Ranking of The Most Influential]." *Wprost*, October 27, 2019. https://www.wprost.pl/tygodnik/10264563/jaroslaw-kaczynski-czyli-naczelnik-naszych-czasow-ranking-najbardziej-wplywowych.html.

———. "Poland Mobilises Controversial 'Weekend Warriors' for Pandemic Response." *Balkan Insight*. November 5, 2020. https://balkaninsight.com/2020/11/05/poland-mobilises-controversial-weekend-warriors-for-pandemic-response/.

Sprenger, Sebastian. "Sweden Clings to Its Non-NATO Status amid Substantial Defense Budget Boost." *Defense News*, April 8, 2021, sec. Europe. https://www.defensenews.com/global/europe/2021/04/08/sweden-clings-to-its-neutrality-amid-substantial-defense-budget-boost/.

Staniland, Paul. "Militias, Ideology, and the State." *Journal of Conflict Resolution* 59, no. 5 (August 1, 2015): 770–93. https://doi.org/10.1177/0022002715576749.

Stegbauer, Andreas. "The Ban of Right-Wing Extremist Symbols According to Section 86a of the German Criminal Code." *German Law Journal* 8, no. 2 (February 1, 2007): 173–84. https://doi.org/10.1017/S2071832200005496.

Stöss, Richard. *Rechtsextremismus im vereinten Deutschland [Right-Wing Extremism in United Germany]*. 2. unveränderte Aufl edition. Bonn: Friedrich-Ebert-Stiftung, Abteilung Dialog Ostdeutschland, 1999.

Strachan, Hew, and Ruth Harris. "The Utility of Military Force and Public Understanding in Today's Britain." Rand Corporation, April 16, 2020. https://www.rand.org/pubs/research_reports/RRA213-1.html.

Sundermeyer, Olaf. *Right-Wing Terror in Germany: A History of Violence.* München: Beck CH, 2012.

Sweden Democrats. "A-Ö [A to Z]." *Sverigedemokraterna* (blog). Accessed July 22, 2021. https://sd.se/a-o/.

Swedish Armed Forces. "The Home Guard's 80th Anniversary." Försvarsmakten. Accessed February 19, 2021. https://www.forsvarsmakten.se/en/news/2020/05/the-home-guards-80th-anniversary/.

Swedish Defense Research Agency (FOI). "Difficult Transition to Democratic Defense," August 25, 2010. https://web.archive.org/web/20100825141814/http://www.foi.se/FOI/templates/Page____560.aspx.

Swedish Security Service. "Swedish Democracy Under Threat on Several Fronts." Text, March 26, 2020. http://www.sakerhetspolisen.se/en/swedish-security-service/about-us/pressroom/current-events/news/2020-03-26-swedish-democracy-under-threat-on-several-fronts.html.

Szczygiel, Konrad. "Millions for Uniforms." *Vsquare.Org*, March 4, 2019. https://vsquare.org/millions-for-uniforms/.

———. "T-Shirts Made in Poland. Not in the European Union." *Vsquare.Org*, January 22, 2019. https://vsquare.org/t-shirts-made-in-poland-not-in-the-eu/.

Tarwacki, Bob. "The Rifleman's Association: Origins and Outcomes of a Nationalistic, Polish Social Movement." City University of New York, 2005. https://www.academia.edu/4434881/The_Riflemans_Association_Origins_and_Outcomes_of_a_Nationalistic_Polish_Social_Movement.

Taussig, Jonathan Katz and Torrey. "An Inconvenient Truth: Addressing Democratic Backsliding within NATO." *Brookings* (blog), July 10, 2018. https://www.brookings.edu/blog/order-from-chaos/2018/07/10/an-inconvenient-truth-addressing-democratic-backsliding-within-nato/.

Teitelbaum, Benjamin R. "In Sweden, Populist Nationalists Won on Policy, but Lost on Politics." The Atlantic, September 12, 2018. https://www.theatlantic.com/ideas/archive/2018/09/in-sweden-populist-nationalists-won-on-policy-but-lost-on-politics/569968/.

Terlecki, Ryszard. *Miecz I Tarcza Komunizmu [The Sword and Shield of Communism]*. Literary Publishing. Accessed May 3, 2021. https://www.amazon.com/tarcza-komunizmu-Polska-wersja-jezykowa/dp/B00C47VUZG/ref=sr_1_3?dchild=1&keywords=Ryszard+Terlecki&qid=1620066111&sr=8-3.

Tomson, Danielle Lee. "The Rise of Sweden Democrats: Islam, Populism and the End of Swedish Exceptionalism." *Brookings* (blog), March 25, 2020. https://www.brookings.edu/research/the-rise-of-sweden-democrats-and-the-end-of-swedish-exceptionalism/.

Trevor-Roper, Hugh. *The Good Old Days: The Holocaust as Seen by Its Perpetrators and Bystanders*. Edited by Ernst Klee, Willi Dressen, and Volker Riess. William S. Konecky Associates, 1996.

Trines, Stefan. "The State of Refugee Integration in Germany in 2019." *World Education News and Reviews*, August 8, 2019. https://wenr.wes.org/2019/08/the-state-of-refugee-integration-in-germany-in-2019.

TRT World. "Merkel Agrees 'Refugee Cap' in Concession to Allies." *TRT World*, October 9, 2017, sec. News. https://www.trt-world.com/europe/merkel-agrees-refugee-cap-in-concession-to-allies-11191.

Warsaw Institute. "Ukrainians Are Getting Armed," August 21, 2018. https://warsawinstitute.org/ukrainians-getting-armed/.

United States Holocaust Memorial Museum. "Kristallnacht." Holocaust Encyclopedia Kristallnacht, October 18, 2019. https://encyclopedia.ushmm.org/content/en/article/kristallnacht.

———. "The SA." Holocaust Encyclopedia The SA, September 17, 2017. https://encyclopedia.ushmm.org/content/en/article/the-sa.

Vasovic, Aleksandar, and Maria Kiselyova. "Russian Forces Seize Two Ukrainian Bases in Crimea." *Reuters*, March 19, 2014. https://www.reuters.com/article/us-ukraine-crisis-idUSBREA2I0TR20140319.

Waite, Robert G. L. *Vanguard of Nazism: The Free Corps Movement in Postwar Germany, 1918-1923*. Harvard University Press, 1952. https://www.hup.harvard.edu/catalog.php?isbn=9780674931428.

Walker, Shaun. "A Whole Generation Has Gone: Ukrainians Seek Better Life in Poland." Guardian, April 18, 2019. http://www.theguardian.com/world/2019/apr/18/whole-generation-has-gone-ukrainian-seek-better-life-poland-elect-president.

Weber, Max, Hans Heinrich Gerth, and C. Wright Mills. *From Max Weber: Essays in Sociology*. Ulan Press, 2012.

Webra International. "The Visegrad Group: Polish Paramilitaries - Training to War in Times of Peace." Text. (C) 2006-2010, International Visegrad Fund, December 9, 2016. https://www.visegradgroup.eu/polish-paramilitaries.

Wegner, Bernd. *Hitlers Politische Soldaten: Die Waffen-SS 1933 - 1945: Leitbild, Struktur und Funktion einer nationalsozialistischen Elite [Hitler's Political Soldiers: The Waffen-SS 1933-1945: Mission, Structure and Function of a National Socialist Elite]*. 8th ed. edition. Schoeningh Ferdinand GmbH, 2010.

Witkowski, Przemyslaw. "In Moscow, the Leader of the Fascist Falanga Calls for Lviv to Join Poland." *OKO Press*, August 30, 2019. https://oko.press/lider-faszyzujacej-falangi-domaga-sie-w-moskwie-przylaczenia-do-polski-lwowa/#.

Yle Uutiset. "Soldiers of Odin's Secret Facebook Group: Weapons, Nazi Symbols and Links to MV Lehti." *Yle Uutiset*, May 17, 2017. https://web.archive.org/web/20170517012354/http://yle.fi:80/uutiset/osasto/news/soldiers_of_odins_secret_facebook_group_weapons_nazi_symbols_and_links_to_mv_lehti/8749308.

Zákony Pro Lidi. "Firearms and Ammunition (Arms Act)." Act No. 119/2002 Coll. Accessed September 16, 2021. https://www.zakonyprolidi.cz/cs/2002-119.

Zemla, Edyta. "Admirałowie Usunięci z Akademii Marynarki Wojennej [Admirals Removed from the Naval Academy]." *Onet Wiadomości*, 39:24 100AD. https://wiadomosci.onet.pl/tylko-w-onecie/admiralowie-usunieci-z-akademii-marynarki-wojennej/q3b710m.

Zetterberg, Kent. "Brother OC Munck." In *Swedish Biographical Dictionary (SBL)*, 773. Accessed February 19, 2021. https://sok.riksarkivet.se/sbl/Presentation.aspx?id=9542.

Ziegler, Herbert F. *Nazi Germany's New Aristocracy: The SS Leadership,1925-1939*. Princeton University Press, 2014.

Zubok, Vladislav M. *A Failed Empire: The Soviet Union in the Cold War from Stalin to Gorbachev*. Paperback edition. Chapel Hill: University of North Carolina Press, 2009.

Carola Hartmann Miles-Verlag

Sicherheitspolitik

Wolf Graf v. Baudissin, *Grundwert: Frieden in Politik – Strategie – Führung von Streitkräften, herausgegeben von Claus von Rosen,* Berlin 2014.

Oliver Schmidt, *Deutsche Außenpolitik und die Zukunft der nuklearen Teilhabe in der NATO,* Berlin 2017.

Dirk Freudenberg, *Theorie des Irregulären – Erscheinungen und Abgrenzungen von Partisanen, Guerillas und Terroristen im Modernen Kleinkrieg sowie Entwicklungstendenzen der Reaktion, (3 Bände),* Berlin 2017.

Markus Reisner, *Robotic Wars – Legitimatorische Grundlagen und Grenzen des Einsatzes von Military Unmanned Systems in modernen Konfliktszenarien,* Berlin 2018.

Helmut Fiedler, *Military Assistance – eine moderne Einsatzart zwischen Anspruch und Wirklichkeit,* Berlin 2019.

Pascal Riemer, *Von der russischen Kriegskunst. Eine Untersuchung der dialektischen Zusammenhänge von Staatsidee und Militärwesen am Beispiel der Sowjetunion und der Russischen Föderation,* Berlin 2021.

Georg Kunovjanek, *Cyber – Die Domäne der vernetzten Unsicherheit. Eine kritische interdisziplinäre Analyse des Krieges der Zukunft und seiner normativen Grundlagen,* Berlin 2021.

Joachim Weber (Hrsg.), *Konfliktraum Arktis. Die Großmächte und der Hohe Norden,* Berlin 2021.

Thomas Jäger, Ralph Thiele (Hrsg.), *Der Politische Islamismus als hybrider Akteur globaler Reichweite. Die liberale demokratische Ordnung muss ihre Resilienz stärken,* Berlin 2021.

Uwe Hartmann, *Die Nato. Mächte und Menschen in der transatlantischen Allianz,* Berlin 2021.

Dirk Freudenberg, *Wehrhaftigkeit der Medienordnung – Rechtliche und rechtspolitische Probleme vor dem Hintergrund der Konzeption Zivile Verteidigung (KZV),* Berlin 2022.

Militär und Gesellschaft

Hans-Christian Beck, Christian Singer (Hrsg.), *Entscheiden – Führen – Verantworten. Soldatsein im 21. Jahrhundert,* Berlin 2011.

Marcel Bohnert, Lukas J. Reitstetter (Hrsg.), *Armee im Aufbruch. Zur Gedankenwelt junger Offiziere in den Kampftruppen der Bundeswehr,* Berlin 2014.

Phil C. Langer, Gerhard Kümmel (Hrsg.), *„Wir sind Bundeswehr." Wie viel Vielfalt benötigen/vertragen die Streitkräfte?,* Berlin 2015.

Eberhard Birk, Peter Andreas Popp (Hrsg.), *Luftwaffenoffizier 21. Das Selbstverständnis des Luftwaffenoffiziers zu Beginn des 21. Jahrhunderts, (aus der Reihe Schriften zur Geschichte der Deutschen Luftwaffe, Band 5),* Berlin 2016.

Alois Bach, Walter Sauer (Hrsg.), *Schützen.Retten.Kämpfen. Dienen für Deutschland,* Berlin 2016.

Marcel Bohnert, Björn Schreiber (Hrsg.), *Die unsichtbaren Veteranen. Kriegsheimkehrer in der deutschen Gesellschaft,* Berlin 2016.

Angelika Dörfler-Dierken (Hrsg.), *Hinschauen! Geschlecht, Rechtspopulismus, Rituale: Systemische Probleme oder individuelles Fehlverhalten?,* Berlin 2019.

Standpunkte und Orientierungen

Uwe Hartmann, *Hybrider Krieg als neue Bedrohung von Freiheit und Frieden. Zur Relevanz der Inneren Führung in Politik, Gesellschaft und Streitkräften,* Berlin 2015.

Martin Sebaldt, *Nicht abwehrbereit. Die Kardinalprobleme der deutschen Streitkräfte, der Offenbarungseid des Weißbuchs und die Wege aus der Gefahr,* Berlin 2017.

Christian J. Grothaus, *Der „hybride Krieg" vor dem Hintergrund der kollektiven Gedächtnisse Estlands, Lettlands und Litauens,* Berlin 2017.

Uwe Hartmann, *Der gute Soldat. Politische Kultur und soldatisches Selbstverständnis heute,* Berlin 2018.

Helmut Jermer, *Innere Führung kompakt. Eine Zusammenschau als Lehr- und Lernhilfe,* Berlin 2019.

Martin Sebaldt, *Das Elend der Strategen. Warum die deutsche Militärpolitik versagt,* Berlin 2020.

Militärgeschichte

Eberhard Kliem, Kathrin Orth, *"Wir wurden wie blödsinnig vom Feind beschossen". Menschen und Schiffe in der Skagerrakschlacht 1916,* Berlin 2016.

Hans Frank, Norbert Rath, *Kommodore Rudolf Petersen. Führer der Schnellboote 1942–1945. Ein Leben in Licht und Schatten unteilbarer Verantwortung,* Berlin 2016.

Eckhard Lisec, *Der Völkermord an den Armeniern im 1. Weltkrieg – Deutsche Offiziere beteiligt?,* Berlin 2017.

Joachim Welz, *Erfolgsstory oder Trauma – die Übernahme von Armeen. Lehren aus der Übernahme des österreichischen Bundesheeres in die Wehrmacht 1938 und der Reste der NVA in die Bundeswehr 1990,* Berlin 2018.

Georg Neuhaus, *Am Anfang war ein Speer. Eine Chronographie der Kriegs- und Militärtechnologien,* Berlin 2018.

Hans-Werner Ahrens, *Die Transportflieger der Luftwaffe 1956 bis 1971. Konzeption – Aufbau – Einsatz, (Reihe Schriften zur Geschichte der Deutschen Luftwaffe, Band 8),* Berlin 2019.

Jobst Reller, *Die Anfänge der evangelischen Militärseelsorge,* Berlin ²2020.

Eberhard Frhr. v. Senden, Friedrich Frhr. v. Senden, *Der Erste Weltkrieg 1914–1918. Erlebnisse eines jungen Leutnants,* Berlin 2020.

Hans-Günter Behrendt, *Flugabwehr in Deutschland. Stationierungsorte und Systeme 1956-2012,* Berlin 2021.

Gerd Bolik, *NATO-Planungen für die Verteidigung der Bundesrepublik Deutschland im Kalten Krieg,* Berlin 2021.

Schriften zur Tradition

Eberhard Birk, Winfried Heinemann, Sven Lange (Hrsg.), *Tradition für die Bundeswehr. Neue Aspekte einer alten Debatte,* Berlin 2012.

Donald Abenheim, Uwe Hartmann (Hrsg.), *Tradition in der Bundeswehr. Zum Erbe des deutschen Soldaten und zur Umsetzung des neuen Traditionserlasses,* Berlin 2018.

Joachim Welz, *Vom Kontingentsheer zum Reichsheer: Militärkonventionen als Motor der Wehrverfassung,* Berlin 2018.

Donald Abenheim, Uwe Hartmann, *Einführung in die Tradition der Bundeswehr. Das soldatische Erbe in dem besten Deutschland, das es je gab,* Berlin 2019.

Eberhard Birk, Heiner Möllers (Hrsg.), *Die Luftwaffe und ihre Traditionen (aus der Reihe Schriften zur Geschichte der Deutschen Luftwaffe, Band 10)*, Berlin 2019.

Hans-Günter Behrendt (Hrsg.): *Erinnerungsorte der Bundeswehr – Personen, Ereignisse und Institutionen der soldatischen Traditionspflege*, Berlin 2020.

Dirk Drews, Stefan Gruhl (Hrsg.): *Oberst Reinhard Hauschild 1921–2005. Traditionsstifter für die Bundeswehr? Gedenkschrift zum 100. Geburtstag*, Berlin 2021.

Dieter Krüger, *Verständigung mit Frankreich. Das vergebliche Plädoyer des Oberst Dr. Hans Speidel. Paris 1940–1942*, Berlin 2021.

Jahrbuch Innere Führung (seit 2009)

Uwe Hartmann, Claus von Rosen (Hrsg.), *Jahrbuch Innere Führung 2019. Bundeswehr im Aufbruch. Hindernisse von den verteidigungspolitischen Vorstellungen der AFD bis zu den sicherheitspolitischen Meinungen in der Zivilgesellschaft*, Berlin 2019.

Uwe Hartmann, Reinhold Janke, Claus von Rosen (Hrsg.), *Jahrbuch Innere Führung 2020. Zur Weiterentwicklung der Inneren Führung: Themen und Inhalte*, Berlin 2020.

Uwe Hartmann, Reinhold Janke, Claus von Rosen (Hrsg.), *Jahrbuch Innere Führung 2021/22. Ein neues Mindset Landes- und Bündnisverteidigung?*, Berlin 2022.

Offiziersbibliothek

Uwe Hartmann, *Offiziersbibliothek I. Deutschland*, Berlin 2020.

Franz H.U. Borkenhagen, Uwe Hartmann, *Offiziersbibliothek II. Internationale Beziehungen und Sicherheitspolitik*, Berlin 2021.

www.miles-verlag.jimdo.com